Instructo

MW00967124

Business Communications

Tom Means

THOMSON
SOUTH-WESTERN

Australia · Canada · Mexico · Singapore · Spain · United Kingdom · United States

THOMSON
SOUTH-WESTERN

Business Communications Instructor's Manual
By Tom Means

Vice President/Editorial Director:
Jack Calhoun

Vice President/Editor-in-Chief:
Dave Shaut

Senior Publisher:
Karen Schmohe

Executive Editor:
Eve Lewis

Project Manager:
Penny Shank

Executive Marketing Manager:
Carol Volz

Senior Marketing Manager:
Nancy A. Long

Marketing Coordinator:
Linda Kuper

Production Editor:
Carol Spencer

Consulting Editor:
Leslie Kauffman

Production Manager:
Patricia Matthews Boies

Manufacturing Coordinator:
Kevin L. Kluck

Design Project Manager:
Tippy McIntosh

Cover Design and Illustration:
Bethany Casey

Internal Design:
Lou Ann Thesing,
Carrie Hochstrasser

Editorial Assistant:
Linda Keith

Production Assistant:
Nancy Stamper

Project Management:
Litten Editing and Production, Inc.

Compositor:
GGS Information Services, Inc.

Printer:

Globus Printing & Packaging

For more information, contact
South-Western
5191 Natorp Boulevard
Mason, OH, 45040.
Or, visit our Internet site at
www.swlearning.com.

For permission to use material from
this text, contact us by

Tel: (800) 730-2214
Fax: (800) 730-2215
Web: www.thomsonrights.com

Introduction

Whether in business or life in general, communication is a crucial part of our lives. Being an effective communicator makes a significant contribution to a contented life. Just the opposite, being an ineffective communicator can result in frustration and disappointment. Because communication is such a vital part of our existence, teaching it in such a way as to help students become effective communicators can be challenging, exciting, and rewarding.

Business Communications is an extremely versatile textbook with outstanding supporting materials that can help you teach this critical subject effectively. Instructors may use this textbook to fit a variety of student abilities and learning situations. The textbook and its accompanying support materials enable you to provide teaching methodologies to accommodate individual student needs. Such a teaching approach usually receives a favorable reaction from students and enhances their learning experience.

This textbook thoroughly covers the basics of workplace communication—letters, memos, e-mail, and reports. Electronic communication, with its increasing importance, receives particular attention. Concepts on electronic communication are presented throughout this textbook. In fact, sections of the text are dedicated to electronic communication and concepts regarding it are integrated throughout the rest of the text, even in a glossary. The text highlights contemporary issues such as ethics, critical thinking, and team projects (for example, collaborative writing). To emphasize the importance of diversity, ethics, and technology, it provides boxed features on these topics. Coverage includes chapters on graphics, technical writing, customer service, researching/ finding and using information, and diversity in the workplace. *Business Communications* also has extensive coverage on the writing of informal and formal reports, resume writing, cover letter writing, interviewing, and other job-getting skills. The text is truly versatile and comprehensive.

Support Materials

We believe that the teaching/learning support materials that accompany *Business Communications* provide a complete, diverse package that will enable you to teach business communication effectively regardless of the type of student. The following items provide a variety of instructional tools:

Title	ISBN
Textbook	0-538-43682-4
Study Guide	0-538-43683-2
Workplace Communication in Action Video with Casebook	0-538-97703-5
Instructor's Resource CD (Includes PowerPoint presentations for each chapter; tests and answer keys for each chapter; transparency masters; instructor's edition of study guide with answers overprinted; and grammar exercises and solutions.)	0-538-43685-9
Exam*View* Electronic Test Bank	0-538-43686-7
Instructor's Manual	0-538-43684-0

Your South-Western Thomson Learning representative will be most happy to help you get any of the materials listed as part of the package.

Course Organization

When planning your course organization, the first objective is to determine course content. *Business Communications* provides a great deal of flexibility. One question you might ask yourself when determining content is, "What kind of communication skills do my students need to develop?"

The following are just a few areas to consider when designing your course:

- **Type of Communication Skill.** What type of communication should be the main focus of the course?
  - written?
  - oral?
  - interpersonal (listening, nonverbal, customer service, diversity in the workplace)?
  - finding and using information?
  - a combination of the above?

- **Formatting Skills.** Do my students need help with the formatting of documents?
  - memos?
  - letters?
  - reports?

- **Job Search Skills.** Do my students need help with their job search skills?
  - resume writing?
  - cover letter writing?
  - interviewing skills?
  - follow-up letter writing?
  - filling out application forms?

- **Other Skill Development.** Should other skills be developed?
  - handling diversity?
  - customer service?
  - technical writing skills?

- **Grammar and Punctuation Skills.** What kind of help do your students need with regards to grammar and punctuation?
  - a review?
  - nothing?

Of course, there are many more specific questions that could be appropriate. The answers to your questions determine the content of your course. For example, if you indicated that your students need to be taught job-getting skills, the amount of course time dedicated to Chapters 14 and 15 would be greater than if you indicated that your students need only a review in these areas. If you indicated that you want to focus on developing their oral communication skills, you would include in your coverage the chapters on speaking

and presenting, customer service, and possibly handling diversity in the workplace.

Business Communications provides many possible combinations for course content. The course you develop should focus on the needs of your students.

Workplace Competencies

The Secretary's Commission on Achieving Necessary Skills (SCANS) Report challenged schools, parents, and businesses to help all students develop the basic skills, thinking skills, personal qualities, and workplace competencies employers require (see the charts below and on the next page).

To prepare for success in the twenty-first century, students need to be taught the SCANS foundation skills and workplace competencies in a way that represents the actual workplace—contextually, within a real environment.

Business Communications gives students many opportunities to practice and develop the SCANS skills and competencies in contextual assignments. Students prepare and deliver written and oral instructions, presentations, and summaries. They compose letters, memos, e-mail, resumes, progress reports, and proposals. The many team activities and chapter projects foster the development of responsibility, self-management, and interpersonal skills, as well as the ability to manage resources effectively. Leadership, decision making skills, and problem-solving skills are presented and applied in group activities.

SCANS FOUNDATION SKILLS	
Competent workers must have:	
Basic Skills	Reading, writing, arithmetic and mathematics, listening, and speaking
Thinking Skills	Creative thinking, decision making, problem solving, processing graphs and symbols, knowing how to learn, and reasoning
Personal Qualities	Responsibility, self-esteem, sociability, self-management, integrity, and honesty

WORKPLACE COMPETENCIES

Effective workers can productively use:

Resources	They know how to allocate time, money, materials, space, and staff.
Interpersonal Skills	They can work on teams, teach others, serve customers, lead, negotiate, and work well with people from diverse backgrounds.
Information	They can acquire and evaluate data, organize and maintain files, interpret and communicate, and use computers to process information.
Systems	They understand social, organizational, and technological systems; they can monitor and correct performance; and they can design or improve systems.
Technology	They can select equipment and tools, apply technology to specific tasks, and maintain and troubleshoot equipment.

Teaching Aids

Take advantage of the many teaching and learning aids *Business Communications* offers. The following features and accompanying support materials will aid you in providing flexibility and variety in your communication classroom:

- **Boxed features.** To emphasize the importance of ethics, diversity, and technology, boxed features are placed in each chapter. Most chapters contain two or three features that introduce to students important concepts about these critical areas.
- **Five types of cases—introductory cases, general cases, career-oriented cases, video cases, and a continuing case.**

    Introductory case. Each chapter in *Business Communications* contains an introductory case and a set of related questions that set the stage for the chapter. Answers to the questions appear at the end of each section, and a case summary appears at the end of the chapter. Use this case to discuss key points throughout the chapter.

    General cases. At the end of each chapter are case studies that require the student to analyze a situation and apply chapter-related skills and concepts.

Career-oriented cases. Career-oriented cases make up part of the end-of-chapter activities for each chapter. These cases focus on a career area and ask students to solve a problem in one of these areas, applying some of the communication concepts taught in the chapter. These career areas include health and human services; business, marketing, and computers; manufacturing, trades, and transportation; agriculture/natural resources; and human/personal services.

Video case. At the end of many chapters, you can use a video case as another teaching/application technique. The video case requires students to analyze a situation related to a *Workplace Communication in Action* video clip in order to solve some problem.

Continuing case. To provide an example of how communication skills are really used in the business world, *Business Communications* provides a continuing case at the end of each chapter. In this case, new business owners are continually called upon to use their communication skills to solve problems that they encounter with customers, suppliers, employees, and silent partners.

- **Team exercises.** One of the most desired skills for employees is the ability to work effectively in teams. To help develop this skill in your students, problems and cases that suggest or require students to collaborate or work in teams are dispersed throughout the text.
- **Key points.** These marginal notations highlight important concepts that are presented in the chapter text.
- **Internet activities.** Throughout the chapter, suggested Internet activities give students the opportunity to develop their online research skills.
- **Illustrations of ineffective/effective documents.** These illustrations appear side-by-side for easy comparison. Callouts within the illustrations highlight key elements in the documents.
- **Writing opportunities.** The abundance of writing opportunities provides constant practice for students.
- **Checkpoints.** Checkpoints within sections of chapters provide constant reinforcement of concepts. Checkpoints solutions located in Appendix E provide immediate feedback.
- **Emphasis on SCANS competencies.** Skills needed to be successful in the workplace are stressed throughout the chapters. Marginal notes next to the chapter content identify the workplace competency being taught.
- **Coordinated chapter objectives.** Chapter objectives are coordinated with the chapter content and chapter summaries and identified with specific icons.
- **Discussion questions.** Discussion questions appear at the end of each section in a chapter. Use these questions to encourage class discussion and assess student comprehension of the section before continuing to the next section within the chapter.
- **Critical thinking questions.** Use these questions to encourage students to expand their thinking about the concepts in the chapter.
- **End-of-chapter applications.** The variety of applications at the end of the chapters provide opportunities for many learning styles. Encourage students to think critically, to apply what they've learned in workplace-related applications, and to capitalize on the use of technology whenever possible.
- **Study Guide assignments.** Use the Study Guide as an excellent review of the chapter material

and as additional writing opportunities. Sample solutions appear in the annotated edition of the Study Guide.
- **PowerPoint presentations.** Use the PowerPoint presentations (available on the Instructor's Resource CD) as an introduction to the content of the chapter or as a review of the chapter before students begin the end-of-chapter applications.
- **Transparency masters.** While the PowerPoint presentations are used most effectively to preview or review a chapter, use the transparency masters (provided in PDF format) to enhance specific concepts in your chapter discussions and to discuss solutions to various applications.
- <u>Workplace Communication in Action</u> **video and casebook.** Video cases appear at the end of many of the chapters. Clips from the video and information in the case are used to solve various communication problems. The Video Casebook includes the cases that appear in the student text as well as additional cases not found in the student text.

Teaching Suggestions

To help both the experienced and new instructor, we offer these teaching suggestions that have proven to be successful in our business communication classrooms. These teaching tips have been found effective through educational research and classroom practice. Select those ideas that are most appropriate for your instructional setting. Chapter-specific suggestions appear in this Instructor's Manual, including chapter outlines that assist with teaching communication concepts and suggest when transparency masters can be used, classroom strategies for teaching specific chapter concepts, and solutions to end-of-chapter activities.

- **Help students recognize the importance of basic communication skills.** The importance of grammar, punctuation, formatting, and planning and organizing should be stressed. Throughout the course, emphasize the importance of planning and organizing each communication—both written and oral.
- **If needed, use Appendix C to review grammar and punctuation skills.** If your students need to improve their grammar and punctuation skills or if they just need a review, use Appendix C. This

appendix provides a brief review of basic grammar and punctuation rules that students must understand and apply. Begin this portion of the course by asking students if they have ever received a written communication full of errors. Ask those who raise their hands to indicate what they thought about the sender of these messages. Their responses should indicate the necessity of these fundamental skills.

- **Stress the importance of quality.** Because every communication situation differs, quality of a communication will depend upon various factors. Help students to realize that one model will not fit all situations. In communications, quality is a moving target that the sender must constantly find. Remind students throughout the course that effective communicators send quality communications.

- **Teach the concepts and then apply.** This text provides a variety of authentic practice throughout. After teaching a concept, make the new material relevant to students by discussing the model documents and examples and by completing the chapter exercises.

- **Integrate marginal notations into class discussions.** The notations provide important points that students will be able to incorporate into their communications. These notations also help students remember key concepts when planning, organizing, or sending communications; they also provide additional bits of helpful information.

- **Use a variety of teaching methods to make your class interesting.** When teaching the class, use as many teaching methodologies as possible. Lecturing is not the best teaching methodology. In fact, research indicates that it is the least effective way to "teach" a class. The more students can experience the principles of effective communication, the easier it will be for them to learn them. For example, when teaching how to operate in groups, divide students into groups and give them an activity. After the activity is over, have them evaluate their group's performance and ask them what they as an individual could have done to make their group more effective.

- **Encourage student participation.** Let students know that the purpose of discussion is to learn by sharing experiences. Stress that effective communicators are those who have learned to be sensitive to subtleties. Thus, the purpose of the class is to learn these subtleties, and participation in the class is an opportunity to share experiences and grow.

  Involve students by discussing critical thinking questions. Use case studies (both the general and career-oriented case studies), projects, letters, memos, oral reports, and written reports to generate discussions. Stress that communication is a dynamic process that requires interaction in order to be successful.

- **Provide feedback.** Students need as many forms of feedback as you can provide. Return tests and other assignments as quickly as possible. In addition to your critique of their assignments, allow students to help evaluate each others' work. If students give oral presentations or are involved in mock job interviews, videotape them and have students evaluate them. When-ever possible, students should edit their documents electronically. Students can participate in peer editing by revising and commenting on each others' work using a word processing package. Word processing allows tracking of edits and the addition of comments, which are embedded in the text. Students then revise their own documents using the edits and comments from their peers.

- **Use transparencies to create additional visual learning experiences.** Additional transparencies may be created from student papers (remove student names) for class critiques. Transparencies of Study Guide activities may be used for discussion and student grading. Students may grade their own papers using the transparencies to give them quick feedback.

- **Use chapter tests to reinforce learning.** You may choose to use the chapter tests provided on the Instructor's Resource CD in PDF format or customize your own tests using the Exam*View* electronic test bank. The Exam*View* electronic test bank contains all questions from the printed test bank and gives you the ability to edit, add, delete, or randomly mix questions.

- **Use Section 5 of Appendix C if you identify weaknesses in spelling and word usage.** The list of commonly confused and misspelled words in Appendix C may be used to test students, enhance class discussion, or supplement chapter tests.

- **Encourage students to use Appendix E: Checkpoint Solutions.** The purpose of the Checkpoints is to assess personal progress as students study each chapter. Immediate feedback reinforces learning and assists students.

Evaluating Student Performance

Feedback is the key to student improvement. Students need feedback; therefore, comments on assignments must be provided. These comments should point out both the weaknesses and the strengths in assignments. When someone does something incorrectly or poorly, tell why it is considered weak or poor, suggest how to correct it, or provide an example of how to correct it. When a student does something well or outstanding, tell him or her so.

Although grading business communications will involve subjectivity, an effective grading system will minimize subjectivity and maximize objectivity. These characteristics will increase student confidence in the grading system and minimize complaints.

To enhance students' confidence in a grading system, explain it to them early in the semester or course term. Consider a grading system composed of objective tests, written applications, and class participation.

Objective Tests

We suggest that objective tests be used to measure students' understanding of the fundamental concepts of business communication. In the test bank, there are 750 true-false, multiple-choice, fill-in-the-blank, and short answer questions. While some of these questions will measure a student's ability to apply a business communication concept, most of them simply measure the student's understanding of a concept. The objective tests provided with *Business Communications* are available in two formats: (1) *ExamView* electronic test bank that allows you to manipulate questions and create tests and (2) Instructor's Resource CD that provides files in PDF format.

Written Applications

Business communication students need the opportunity to apply concepts learned. Applications require them to write or to give oral presentations. These assignments include letters, memos, reports, e-mails, newsletters, web pages, proposals, resumes, and oral

presentations of every kind. Applications may include end-of-chapter applications, case studies, Study Guide activities, or something created by the instructor. Some of these assignments should be completed in class, and some should be out of class.

When giving assignments, remind students that the following process can help them to construct effective communications:

1. Plan communications using the four-step process:
   a. Identify the objective.
   b. Determine the main idea.
   c. Choose supporting information.
   d. Adjust the message for the receiver.
2. Organize communications.
3. Set aside and then rewrite if necessary.
4. Use editing skills.
5. Use a correct format.
6. Use the appropriate checklist to aid in the writing process.

Class Participation

Class participation can be part of a student's grade or it can be used simply to determine if students understand the material being presented. Keys to measuring student understanding of communication concepts are student responses to the following support materials:

- Chapter cases
- Marginal notations
- Video cases
- Discussion questions
- Critical thinking questions
- Transparencies
- PowerPoint presentations

Part of students' grades could be based on class participation. However, realize that this part of the grade would be viewed by students as entirely subjective.

Summary

Business Communications was developed with the instructor and student in mind. In the workplace, communication is a critical, much-valued skill. While there is no set formula for an effective business communication course, we have presented some ideas that have helped us to be more effective in the classroom. Enhance the probability of effective instruction by

- Organizing the course to meet the needs of your students.
- Teaching the course using effective methodologies.
- Evaluating students so that they perceive you are fair and objective.

Business Communications, with its accompanying package, provides effective tools for teaching, learning, and applying communication concepts—the ingredients for the development of effective communication skills.

Electronic Media
Limited Warranty

South-Western Educational and Professional Publishing ("South-Western") extends the following warranty to only the original customer:

Warranty Coverage

This warranty covers the media on which the South-Western software/data are recorded. This limited warranty does not extend to the information contained on the media and in the accompanying book materials (the "Software/data"). The media product is warranted against malfunction due to defective materials or construction. This warranty is void if the media product is damaged by accident or unreasonable use, neglect, installation, improper service, or other causes not arising out of defects in material or construction.

Warranty Duration

The media product is warranted for a period of three months from the date of the original purchase by the customer.

Warranty Disclaimers

The following should be read and understood before purchasing and/or using the media:

a. Any implied warranties that arise out of this sale are limited in duration to the above three-month period. South-Western will not be liable for loss of use of the media or other incidental or consequential costs, expenses, or damages incurred by you, the consumer, or any other user. Furthermore, South-Western will not be liable for any claim of any kind whatsoever by any other party against the user of the Software/data.

b. South-Western does not warrant that the Software/data and the media will be free from error or will meet the specific requirements of the consumer. You, the consumer, assume complete responsibility for any decisions made or actions taken based on information obtained using the Software/data.

c. Any statements made concerning the utility of the Software/data are not to be construed as expressed or implied warranties.

d. SOUTH-WESTERN MAKES NO WARRANTY, EITHER EXPRESSED OR IMPLIED, INCLUDING BUT NOT LIMITED TO ANY IMPLIED WARRANTY OR MERCHANTABILITY AND FITNESS FOR A PARTICULAR PURPOSE, REGARDING THE SOFTWARE/ DATA AND MAKES ALL SOFTWARE/ DATA AVAILABLE SOLELY ON AN "AS IS" BASIS.

e. In no event will South-Western be liable to anyone for special collateral, incidental, or consequential damages in connection with or arising out of the purchase or use of the Software/data. The sole and exclusive liability of South-Western, regardless of the form of action, will not exceed the purchase price of the media.

f. Some states do not allow the exclusion or limitation of implied warranties or consequential damages, so the above limitations or exclusions may not apply to you in those states.

Further Disclaimers of Warranty

South-Western will extend no warranty where the software is used on a machine other than that designated on the software package.

Media Replacement

Provided that you, the customer, have satisfactorily completed and returned a copy of the License Agreement, South-Western will replace, during the warranty period, any defective media at no charge. At South-Western's option, the defective media must be returned, postage prepaid, along with proof of purchase date. Please contact South-Western at the address shown below for return instructions before returning any defective media.

> South-Western
> Media Services
> 5191 Natorp Boulevard
> Mason, OH 45040

Legal Remedies

This warranty gives you specific legal rights, and you may also have other rights that vary from state to state.

Technical Support Hotline

The Technical Support Hotline is available by phone, fax, or e-mail from 8:30 a.m.–6:00 p.m. EST to help you with any technical problems you may be having with this media product.

Phone: 1-800-423-0563
Fax: 859-647-5045
E-mail: support@kdc.com (24-hour response)

If you identify a problem, please check your hardware to make sure it is working properly. If the hardware is functioning correctly, call the number given. Please have the following information and materials with you when calling the hotline:

*   Program or data CD-ROM
*   Text

*   Instructor's manual
*   List of any error messages
*   Students' printouts
*   Description of the problem
*   Computer type and model
*   Computer's memory configuration
*   Version number of operating system
*   Name and version number of commercial software (if applicable)

Please do not permit your students access to the hotline contact information. If you want to order software, call Thomson Learning at (800) 354-9706.

RESOURCES LIST for
Business Communications, 1e

	Study Guide	Test Bank	Transparency Masters	PowerPoint	Video	Video Casebook
Chapter 1	✓	✓	✓	✓	✓	✓
Chapter 2	✓	✓	✓	✓	✓	✓
Chapter 3	✓	✓	✓	✓	✓	✓
Chapter 4	✓	✓	✓	✓		
Chapter 5	✓	✓	✓	✓	✓	✓
Chapter 6	✓	✓	✓	✓	✓	✓
Chapter 7	✓	✓	✓	✓	✓	✓
Chapter 8	✓	✓	✓	✓	✓	✓
Chapter 9	✓	✓	✓	✓		
Chapter 10	✓	✓	✓	✓	✓	✓
Chapter 11	✓	✓	✓	✓	✓	✓
Chapter 12	✓	✓	✓	✓	✓	✓
Chapter 13	✓	✓	✓	✓	✓	✓
Chapter 14	✓	✓	✓	✓		
Chapter 15	✓	✓	✓	✓		

CONTENTS

Chapter 1 Communicating in Your Life

Student Learning Objectives

Section 1
- List the purposes of communication.
- Diagram the communication process and identify its main points.
- List the two media used for sending messages and the two media used for receiving messages.

Section 2
- List the three major responsibilities of senders and two major responsibilities of receivers.
- Define the forms of communication.
- List the two types of barriers to communication and provide examples.

Section 3
- Identify equipment and software used to create and edit documents.
- Identify technologies used to send and store documents electronically.
- Identify technologies used to send oral messages electronically.

Teaching Outline

Introductory Points
- Communication is a process.
- We spend most of our time communicating.
- Language is a major tool used when communicating.
- Your success in life is dependent upon your communication skills.

I. Communication's Importance and Roles in Your Life—Emphasize that everything we do sends a message—whether intended or not. The challenge for us is to send the messages that will make us effective.

A. Purposes of Communication
1. To establish and build goodwill
   a. Goodwill is the favorable reputation an individual or company has and develops.
   b. An example of goodwill—a congratulations on an anniversary.
2. To persuade—example: a salesperson in a store trying to get the customer to buy a new clothes dryer.
3. To obtain and share information—example: a supervisor telling his or her subordinates of a new company policy.
4. To establish personal effectiveness—example: a student demonstrating his or her skills on a test.
5. To build self-esteem—example: an interviewee telling an interviewer of his or her abilities.

B. Components of the Communication Process
1. The sender—the person or thing that originates a message and initiates the communication process. In the communication process, this person has the greatest challenge!
2. The message—a set of symbols that make up an idea or concept—symbols may be verbal or nonverbal.
   a. verbal symbols—words used in spoken or written messages. (Use Transparencies 1-1 and 1-2 here.)
   b. nonverbal symbols—examples of nonverbal symbols are gestures, posture, facial expressions, appearance, time, tone of voice, eye contact, and space.
   c. If verbal and nonverbal symbols disagree, receivers generally believe the message of the nonverbal symbols.
3. The receiver—the person or thing to whom a message is sent. The receiver is the key to effective communication. If he or she fails to get the message, the sender fails.
4. Feedback—the receiver's response to a message. The sender needs to use this part of the communication process to make sure that the receiver has understood the message sent.

5. Channel—the mode senders select to send a message. Channel can be critical when the sender is trying to ensure that his or her message is interpreted accurately.
C. Communication Media
1. Speaking—over a period of time, helps to create your image
2. Writing—least used communication media
3. Reading—a major part of every job
4. Listening—the most frequently used communication media
II. Communication: Responsibilities of Participants, Forms, and Barriers
A. Responsibilities of Participants
1. Sender
a. Audience analysis (The skill to analyze the audience accurately is a key to the sender's ability to communicate effectively.)
i. background
ii. interests
iii. attitudes
iv. emotional state
b. Message environment
c. Soliciting feedback (Use Transparency 1-3 here.)
2. Receiver
a. Reading
b. Listening
B. Forms of Communication
1. External and internal
2. Formal and informal
3. Written, oral, and electronic
C. Barriers to Communication—Use Transparency 1-4 here. Effective communicators learn to anticipate barriers and avoid them.
1. External
2. Internal
III. Electronic Communication
A. Creating and Editing a Document—This process is becoming easier. In the near future, we will have voice dictation as a means of creating and editing a document.
1. Creating a document—hardware
a. Computers
b. Electronic workstations
c. Scanners
d. Voice recognition equipment

2. Editing a document—software
a. Word processing software
b. Integrated software packages
c. Spreadsheet software
d. Database management software
e. Graphics software
f. Desktop publishing software
B. Sending a Document Electronically—This electronic transfer is already so quick that the time needed to transfer a document is usually unnoticeable.
1. Networks
a. Office
b. Local area
c. Wide area
2. Electronic mail—Use Transparency 1-5 here. E-commerce uses e-mail as a means of conducting business—buying and selling using the Internet. It is growing very quickly and is a major competition to the traditional way we buy and sell items.
3. File transfer protocol
4. Fax machine
C. Storing a Document
1. Magnetic disks
2. Microforms
3. Optical disks
D. Sending Electronic Oral Messages
1. Pagers
2. Cellular phones
3. Voice mail
4. Teleconferences and videoconferences

Classroom Strategies

The content of this first chapter is critical. If students understand the importance of communication in their lives, they will be more dedicated to learning the concepts of this course. But before they can improve their communication skills, they need to understand what communication is. Then concepts such as audience analysis, channel selection, and message environment become important facets of the communication process rather than just concepts.

Use the end-of-chapter activities to review the content of the chapter. Use the cases to stimulate discussion of the importance of communication, the communication process, and electronic communication in the workplace. These activities also illustrate that the environment of a message influences the content and timing of a message.

Solutions to End-of-Section Activities

Discussion Questions

Section 1.1

1. All five of the purposes of communication are equally important. Without any of them, we could not be effective individuals.
2. There are several interpretations: (1) the receiver did not hear the message, (2) the receiver does not want to respond to the message, (3) the receiver wants the sender to think he or she is ignoring the sender, or (4) the receiver is thinking about the response before expressing it. These are four interpretations but there may be others possible.
3. Answers to this question will vary. But the amount of time allocated to their teaching will probably not reflect the usage of the media.

Section 1.2

1. All three are equally important. Audience analysis is important because it analyzes the receiver and provides information about possible adjustments the sender may need to make to his or her message. Message environment is important because it tells the sender if he or she should send the message at this time. Soliciting feedback is important because it tells the sender about his or her relationship with the receiver and if he or she needs to change that relationship.
2. Use a letter to send a message to someone outside your organization. Use a memo to send a message to someone inside your organization. Use an oral message to send an informal or personal message to a receiver.
3. The challenge for the extrovert is to think before speaking. The challenge for the introvert is to make sure he or she speaks.

Section 1.3

1. The following are used for the creation of a document:
    a. computerized workstation with software
    b. scanner
    c. voice recognition equipment
2. Word processing software enables text to be entered, formatted, revised, and printed efficiently. Integrated software permits the user to use word processing, spreadsheets, database, and graphics software simultaneously. Spreadsheet software produces an electronic worksheet used for preparing and analyzing financial records, such as budgets, inventories, and payrolls. Database management software provides a way to store and retrieve information electronically. Graphics software is used to analyze data and make visual aids for presentations. Desktop publishing software enables a personal computer and a high-quality printer to produce documents of typeset quality.
3. Teleconferencing and videoconferencing are becoming more popular because the cost of an employee's time and the cost of travel (airfares and lodging) are becoming increasingly expensive.

Solutions to End-of-Chapter Activities

Critical Thinking Questions

1. Communication is important in every job. It is used by your supervisors to evaluate your attitude toward your job. If they perceive your attitude to be good, then you will receive the benefits of that perception; if they perceive it to be bad, you will also receive the problems related to that perception.
2. In the communication process, the receiver is more in control than the sender because the receiver can better control the effectiveness of his or her actions—effective listening and effective reading. The sender, on the other hand, has a much more difficult, sometimes complex, assessment to make. He or she must determine the symbols needed to make the message understandable. This action requires analyzing the receiver (audience analysis), analyzing and judging the message's environment, and understanding his or her relationship with the receiver and making the necessary adjustments to the message. All of the sender's responsibilities are dependent upon his or her assessment of others.
3. If you are up-to-date on electronic communication equipment and software, you will be better able to select an effective message channel. Also, you should be able to be more efficient in the use of the time needed to compose and send a message.

4. Message environment should tell you when to send a message. It can also tell you whether to send a formal message or an informal one.
5. A pager tells the receiver that he or she has a message. A cellular phone is a portable telephone that enables the receiver to receive a phone call while away from the traditional telephone.

Applications

Part A. The degree of importance for each medium of communication will vary because of the job situation. However, all four mediums—speaking, writing, listening, and reading—may be important. For example, if you were a bus driver, speaking would be important because you would be answering people's questions and giving directions. Writing would not be as important as speaking. However, when the driver has to fill out a report, writing would be important. Listening would be important because, in order to answer questions or give directions, the driver must understand people's questions. Reading would be important because it could be a means of training or gaining information to share with riders of the bus.

Part B. The answer to this question will vary with the individual. For example, quiet, shy individuals should indicate that a major barrier to communication is their fear of speaking. However, they might say that they listen well most of the time. In fact, they might say that the only time they have a problem listening is when they are ill.

Editing Activities
In the solutions, words and punctuation that contained errors in the original paragraphs are underlined.

1. Just as the Earth's waters are made up of various oceans, seas, and lakes, so too is the Internet composed of various networks, ranging from the large (governments and multinational corporations) to the middling (educational institutions and medium-sized businesses) to the small (nonprofit organizations and small businesses). In turn, these networks are connected together via cables and telephone trunk lines that are not unlike waterways and channels that connect the oceans, seas, and lakes.
2. The big difference between navigating the seas and navigating the Internet is the speed of the journey. An around-the-world cruise, for example, might take weeks, but a file or e-mail note can easily go around the globe in just a few seconds. Thanks to the connections between networks, those that travel on the Net, unlike their seafaring counterparts, can travel thousands of miles per second without leaving their chairs. You can go from California to Australia, pick up a file, copy it to London and Frankfurt, and do it all before your coffee gets cold.

Case Studies
1. Situation A
   a. A good use of e-mail—when an individual needs to get information to someone quickly.
   b. A bad use of e-mail—when an individual needs to ask the boss for a day off. This message needs to be delivered face-to-face.

   Situation B — Yes, this factor does impact your decision. You should delay sending the e-mail. The message environment is not yet correct.
2. Yes, you should contact him. For the sake of speed and because you have just personally visited him, you should probably e-mail him first. After a couple of days, you might telephone him and ask him if he received your e-mail. If he indicates that he did, you might say something like "I just wanted to be sure that you are able to take advantage of the sale." If he did not receive the e-mail, you should tell him about the sale and that you will send him the appropriate literature.

Career Case Studies

Communication for Health Services Careers
1. In Samantha's present job, communication is important. She must talk with patients and doctors, loved ones, and other nurses. Also, she has to record critical information such as medicines administered and changes in patients' progress.
2. In the position offered to Samantha, communication is important. She would have to communicate with doctors, nurses in the wing who report to her, loved ones, and her supervisors. She would be more responsible for effective communication within the wing.

3. In the supervisory job, Samantha would have to communicate so as to motivate the nurses under her. In her present job, motivation is not part of her responsibilities.

4. Yes, the difference should be an important part of her consideration. If she does not have the communication skills necessary to motivate those under her supervision, Samantha should not take the position.

Communication for Engineering and Industrial Careers

1. Alex should tell his supervisor that he wishes to be considered in the future for promotion, and he should share his educational plans and goals.

2. In Alex's situation, communication is important. It is used by management to determine Alex's feelings about his job. To be a good candidate for promotion, Alex needs to demonstrate the communication skills needed by a supervisor. He can also volunteer for committees or special tasks that will provide him with experience or new skills.

Video Case

1. Andre should examine his own communication skills. Ms. Slansky and the DTS both presented information to Andre, but he either thought it did not pertain to his job search or that he did not need the information until later. Ms. Slansky indicated she was in a big hurry, but Andre ignored that communication.

2. Sandy was not only persistent, he was also an effective communicator. For example, Sandy was a good listener. He applied what he learned from the Human Resources manager. For example, he moved to New York. When Ken Krupka told Sandy he needed someone organized, Sandy made sure Ken knew he was very organized. In addition, Sandy impressed upon Ken his love of science fiction, to the point of including a promotion for the Sci-Fi Network in his demo tape.

3. Student answers will vary. Andre certainly fell short in establishing and building goodwill. He also seemed unable to persuade the Sci-Fi staff that he was the correct choice for the job opening. Andre's choice of sample tape failed to establish personal effectiveness. Finally, Andre's inconsistent listening skills compromised his ability to obtain or share information.

4. Student ideas will vary. The important thing is that students listen attentively, in order to accurately repeat what they have heard.

Continuing Case

1. Eva and Ramon will communicate with each other and with customers mostly by speaking. They will use written communications with customers in the form of advertising and monthly bills. They will communicate with suppliers through written orders and with their silent partners through oral and written reports. Eva will keep up-to-date by reading. The partners must listen carefully to each other so they can work together. They must listen to customers so they can meet their needs.

2. With her uncle: different personalities, ages, backgrounds, knowledge, and experiences. With customers: all of the above, plus different levels of computer knowledge, different comfort levels in dealing with technology, and different cultures.

3. Possible answers: dealing with computer-phobic customers; becoming aware of, purchasing, and learning how to use the latest technology; dealing with technological glitches.

4. Students should be able to express clearly their own opinions and accurately summarize their partners' opinions. Conditions that might make this exercise more difficult: the partners disagree; one or both feel uncomfortable in sharing their opinions; one or both express their opinions too aggressively; different language backgrounds; an atmosphere that is too noisy, warm, crowded, or otherwise uncomfortable; time constraints.

Chapter 2
Communicating in a Diverse Workplace

Student Learning Objectives

Section 1
- Define "cultural diversity," "multicultural," and "multinational."
- List population trends that indicate the U.S. workplace is becoming more multicultural.
- Identify three projections for the global workplace of the twenty-first century.
- List, describe, and give examples of differences among cultures.

Section 2
- Define "cross-cultural communication."
- List and explain four guidelines to help people communicate effectively across cultures.
- Identify strategies for effective global communication.

Section 3
- List benefits of diversity in the workplace.
- Recognize types of diversity in the workplace and understand the challenges diversity creates.
- Use communication tips for handling diversity.

Section 4
- Identify five stages in effective team development.
- Name and describe five roles needed for effective teams.
- List qualities shared by successful teams.
- Define "virtual team."

Teaching Outline

Introductory Points
- Workers in the United States are increasingly likely to encounter people from cultures different from their own.
- Communicating with people from different cultures presents special challenges and takes special skills.
- Workplace diversity is more than cultural; it encompasses race, gender, age, and ability.
- To work effectively in teams, team members must adopt team goals and carry out team roles.

I. Cultural Differences at Home and Abroad
   A. Cultural Diversity
   B. The World as a Global Workplace
      1. A multinational company not only does business in two or more nations, it also develops a multinational workforce.
      2. Global interaction occurs on a daily basis.
      3. Changing technology will make global business all the more common in the coming century.
   C. Cultural Differences
      1. Though English is relatively widely studied, most people in the world do not understand it. (Use Transparency 2-1.)
      2. Body language is interpreted differently in different parts of the world. (Use Transparency 2-2.)
      3. The amount of eye contact considered appropriate during a conversation varies from culture to culture.
      4. Personal space preferences vary among people of different cultures.
      5. People from some cultures place great significance on the exchange of business cards.

II. Effective Cross-Cultural Communication
   A. Communicating Across Cultures
      1. Guidelines for cross-cultural communication
         a. Learn about and accept cultural differences.
         b. Be sensitive toward people from other cultures.
         c. Be prepared for language barriers—and get past them. (Use Transparency 2-3.)
         d. Keep messages simple and short.
      2. Strategies for global communication
         a. Be adaptable.
         b. Use your best English-speaking habits.
         c. Do not use acronyms, slang, and jargon.
         d. Be aware of a culture's forms of nonverbal communication.
         e. Use visual aids.

f. Recognize that people from cultures other than your own have different assumptions.

g. Be careful about using humor.

h. Maintain personal contact.

III. Other Diversities in the Workplace

A. Benefits of Diversity

1. A diverse group of employees is considered an asset.

2. Recognizing diversity can help coworkers work together more smoothly and more productively.

B. Challenges of Diversity

1. Types of diversity include race or ethnicity, gender, physical abilities, social class, age, socioeconomic status, religion, and personality.

2. Stereotypes lead us to judge people as members of a group rather than as individuals.

C. Diversity Tips (Use Transparency 2-4.)

1. Remember that diversity has many levels and complexities, including cultures within cultures.

2. Don't separate people from the group.

3. Admit what you don't know.

4. Notice what people call themselves.

5. Don't make assumptions based on a person's appearance, name, or group.

6. Don't patronize people.

7. Don't doubt the authenticity of what you hear.

8. Be willing to have your biases changed.

9. When writing, replace judgments with facts.

10. When writing and speaking, consider whether some references and adjectives should be deleted.

11. Use parallel titles and terms.

12. Think about your use of "we."

13. Do not use judgmental words.

14. When writing, have someone review your work who may have a different perspective.

IV. Working Effectively in Teams

A. Workplace Teams

1. Workplace teams are a trend in American companies.

2. Some teams are more effective than others.

B. Effective Work Teams (Use Transparency 2-5.)

1. Work teams evolve into productive groups; they don't just "happen."

2. Most teams go through five stages of development, during which team members get acquainted, establish their roles, and develop a team identity.

3. Team members fulfill various roles to help the team function. (Use Transparency 2-6.)

4. Effective teams have certain characteristics in common.

a. Members are supportive of each other and have a shared team vision.

b. Team members try to improve performance, and they review both successes and failures.

c. Team members recognize and talk about their differences.

C. Virtual Teams

1. Members of a virtual team do not share physical work space, but use communications technology to collaborate.

2. Working in a virtual team presents particular challenges because of the forms of communication the team members use, such as faxes, e-mail, and videoconferencing.

Classroom Strategies

Encourage students to draw from their own experiences as they read this chapter. Recognizing diversity among classmates, school personnel, local businesspeople, and their own employers and coworkers is the first step toward handling diversity effectively. From there, students can apply what they've learned to the workplaces they will enter later in life.

Refer students to the web sites discussed in the feature on page 41. They may serve as valuable resources as students explore the issue of workplace diversity.

Students likely have had experience working in groups or on teams. Again, have them draw on this experience and analyze what they could have done differently to make their teams more productive or efficient.

Solutions to End-of-Section Activities

Discussion Questions

Section 2.1

1. Tens of thousands of immigrants come to the United States each year, creating a more culturally mixed workforce than ever before. In addition, it is easier than ever to do business with people on the other side of the world. Students may cite cultural diversity that they see in their classes, at their workplaces, or in other community organizations or establishments.

2. A smile in America usually means friendliness or understanding. In other cultures, a person may smile out of shyness, embarrassment, lack of understanding, or simply to avoid creating conflict. The American "OK" sign means "worthless" in France, and is an obscene gesture in other cultures.

3. Personal space is the area immediately around a person. Everyone has a certain distance at which they are comfortable speaking with casual acquaintances. Americans' personal space is about 18 inches to 3 feet. Some peoples, such as those of Hispanic heritage, have a smaller personal space. Other cultures, generally more formal, have a larger personal space and feel crowded or insulted if someone stands closer than about 3 feet.

4. The recipient should take the card with both hands and examine it at some length, then keep it nearby during a meeting, for reference. Do not simply glance at the card or tuck it away immediately into a pocket or briefcase.

Section 2.2

1. Cross-cultural communication occurs when people who are not from the same culture attempt to communicate. Communication barriers exist when people of diverse cultures communicate. Barriers may take the form of differences in language or fluency, or differences in beliefs, ways of thinking, values, customs, and so on.

2. Slang, jargon, and abbreviations are particularly difficult to understand for someone who is not thoroughly acquainted with the English language and/or American culture.

3. Learning about another culture might help you understand how people make decisions, why they allow a long silence after you say something, or what is important to them. In short, learning about people helps us understand them and feel more comfortable around them—making it easier to communicate.

4. Students may list any five of the following: be adaptable; use your best English; do not use acronyms, slang, and jargon; be aware of a culture's forms of nonverbal communication; use visual aids; recognize that people from cultures other than your own have different assumptions; be careful about using humor; and maintain personal contact. Explanations should be logical.

Section 2.3

1. Different people have different skills and talents to lend to various workplace situations. Combining those skills makes for a more interesting and a more productive organization.

2. Students may name ethnic background or race, gender, physical ability, educational background or training, social class, age, socioeconomic status, religion, personality, and so on. Workers of diverse backgrounds have to accept each other as individuals, with unique skills and attributes, rather than as members of a group. Workers must adapt their work and communication styles to complement those of their coworkers.

3. Don't stereotype or lump people into groups whose members all have certain characteristics. Don't make assumptions or judge based on a person's name or appearance. Accept other people as authorities, and don't patronize them. Avoid biased or judgmental terms when writing or speaking, and so on.

Section 2.4

1. Team 1 takes advantage of each member's strengths. The members also share common (i.e., team) goals and identify with the team.

2. Students may agree or disagree. Some may say that the stages sound time-consuming and, therefore, do not happen in the rush of getting business done.

3. Students have likely been part of teams at one time or another. Success or lack thereof likely had to do with working as a team rather than as a number of individuals, recognizing and sharing team goals, working together instead of against each other, and so on.

Solutions to End-of-Chapter Activities

Critical Thinking Questions

1. People from diverse cultures differ in terms of customs, values, manners, perceptions, social structure, decision-making practices, and in the language they use, both verbal and nonverbal.
2. We can communicate more effectively with people from other cultures by not making assumptions about the people as a group; by not stereotyping them; by being sensitive to issues of religion, customs, and traditions; and by being respectful and conservative in our actions so as not to offend.
3. Diversity in the American workplace will increase as immigrants pour into the United States. Though they become U.S. citizens, they may still have cultural differences with other Americans. We can prepare by becoming multilingual, as many immigrants are, and by accepting people from other cultures.
4. Other types of diversity have to do with socioeconomic status, physical ability, and personality in general. These types of diversity also need sensitivity. Effective workers need to treat each coworker as a valued individual.
5. Students should identify their personal strengths. They may mention the stages of team development or the team roles as they explain how to improve an ineffective team.

Applications

Part A. Students may consult electronic or print sources for information about specific cultures. In particular, they should focus on the business practices of the nation they chose. Students' suggestions for simplifying communication may involve simply getting to know the person, showing the person around the office or around town, having the person explain how he or she likes to work, and so on. Accept any idea that involves dealing with the person as an equal and showing respect for the person's differences.

Part B. Students' plans should consider all types of diversity, not just cultural. Ideas for training delivery should include all levels of employees. Students may suggest that an outside firm or consultant be hired to deliver the training so that employees are more open

to the information. It would probably be best to avoid having upper management issue memos or hold seminars.

Part C. The work plan should have logical and realistic goals, given the time required in initial meetings for getting acquainted, becoming accustomed to each other's working styles, and assuming team roles.

Part D. Letters of application should demonstrate students' awareness of cultural differences and how to communicate effectively in spite of them.

Editing Activity

[Corrected words or phrases are underlined.]

As most of <u>you are</u> aware, June 14th–16th <u>are the dates</u> on which our colleagues from Indonesia will visit. They will be in the office shadowing <u>individuals</u> from each department<u>.</u> As our main distributor in Asia, Emarnco is <u>very</u> important to us. We want our visitors to feel good about our products as well as about <u>the people</u> who make them. For that reason, following are some reminders to help you make a good impression on and communicate effectively with our visitors.

1. Our guests are native Malays and prefer to be called that. Do <u>not</u> call them Asians or Indonesians.
2. People from the Indonesian culture are <u>comfortable</u> with silence. If you ask a <u>question</u>, give the person time <u>to</u> answer. Indonesians consider it polite to leave a respectful pause before <u>responding</u>.
3. In general, while our guests are here, plan to spend more time being a host or hostess than working. Showing respect, being polite, and not being hurried or rushed are all important to Indonesians. For that reason, it may seem as if you spend a great deal of time being introduced and making the acquaintance of <u>the</u> visitors. Don't feel that you need to look especially <u>busy</u> or productive to <u>impress</u> them. They are here to get acquainted, not to check our production schedules.

Case Studies

1. Students' answers will vary, but should include an acknowledgment that Elaine likely misinterpreted her client's gesture. Mexicans beckon with the palm facing outward, rather than inward, as Americans do.

2. Students' answers will vary, but should include discussion of the following: lack of getting-acquainted period, the inclusion of all team members, the clear establishment of team goals as well as individual tasks, and leadership style. Some students may also speculate about gender bias on the part of Carlos.
3. Student answers will vary.

Career Case Studies

Communication for Natural Resources and Agricultural Careers

Students' suggestions will vary. They should recognize, however, that Jill and the rest of her staff need to stop lumping the seasonal workers into a group. Everyone, including Jill, needs to think of them as individuals. Someone in the office, perhaps Jill or the office manager, should do some significant research about the country or countries where the workers came from. Those countries may have completely different rules or customs, which would account for some apparent misunderstandings about taxes and payroll withholdings.

Video Case

1. Yes, Oliver seems to lack experience with female engineers and with someone of another culture. Oliver seems judgmental and makes sweeping racial and gender generalizations. ("All Asians, particularly women, are retiring and nonconfrontational.") Students may note that more exposure in the workplace to men and women of differing backgrounds might sensitize Oliver. The perceptive student may note that creating a diverse workplace at Millennium Design appears more complicated than hiring more female engineers.
2. Perhaps Emily is simply shy or embarrassed by praise. Her reactions may stem from her cultural background or from her unique personality or a combination of both. Emily's theory of management may differ from Oliver's, and this may drive her actions more than gender or race.

3. As Oliver, a student might describe that he is uncomfortable around Emily, that he does not understand her management style, that he is confused by her seeming disinterest in praise, and (perhaps more to the point) that he doesn't feel she appreciates the praise and support he has shown her. As Emily, a student might ask that she be evaluated on her results, not on her personality. Emily might explain her reasons for appearing shy, especially when faced with praise, or she might simply stress her commitment to her group, department, and company.
4. Team approaches and statements will vary.

Continuing Case

1. He assumes she is quite laid back and unconcerned about time and schedules—a stereotype of Puerto Ricans.
2. Students' answers will vary. They may believe that the salesman was influenced by one or all of the factors listed, but they should give logical reasons to support their opinions.
3. Possible examples: a teenager assumes that all teenagers like rock music; an elderly woman assumes that all elderly women prefer quiet, sedentary activities; a member of a group assumes that all members of that group feel persecuted by other groups. People in any group can hold mistaken ideas about others within and outside their group. Prejudice has no boundaries.
4. Students' letters should politely explain that Eva is concerned about her new business opening on time and providing all the services she has advertised. Students might add that Eva is proud of her cultural background, but Mr. Colon should not make assumptions about her—or anyone else—based on that background.

Chapter 3 Nonverbal Communication

Student Learning Objectives

Section 1

1. Describe the roles of nonverbal communication.
2. Discuss nonverbal symbols in differing cultural and international settings.
3. Indicate the nonverbal symbols sent in written messages.
4. List nonverbal symbols sent in spoken messages.
5. Explain why nonverbal communication is important to you.
6. Describe nonverbal symbols in the environment.

Section 2

1. Discuss the listening process and the types of listening.
2. Identify the reasons for and the benefits of listening.
3. List the barriers to effective listening.
4. Describe effective listening techniques.

Teaching Outline

Introductory Points

- Nonverbal communication is composed of messages we send without or in addition to words.
- Understanding nonverbal communication is an *extremely important* skill that we use when interpreting messages.
- Receivers use their senses when trying to understand nonverbal symbols.
- We spend more time listening than in any other communication activity.
- We remember only about one-half to one-fourth of what we hear.

I. Nonverbal Communication: A Key to Accurate Communication
  A. The Roles of Nonverbal Communication
    1. Reinforcing the verbal message: Example—we shake our heads up and down while saying yes.
    2. Contradicting the verbal message: Example—we say that he is a very good worker while using a sarcastic tone.
    3. Substituting for the verbal message: Example—You stand by the side of the road with your arm out and your thumb extended to signal that you want a ride.
    4. Regulating the verbal message: Example—We signal a question by raising the pitch of our voice at its end.
  B. Nonverbal Symbols in Differing Cultural and International Settings—Use the experiences of students in your class that use English as a second langauge. Ask them about differences in the meanings of nonverbal symbols—Example: In Greece, the up and down movement of the head means *no*.
  C. Nonverbal Symbols in Written Messages (Use Transparencies 3-1 and 3-2 here.)
  D. Nonverbal Symbols in Spoken Messages
    1. Body language
      a. Facial expressions
      b. Gestures
    2. Touching
    3. Space
      a. Intimate zone
      b. Personal zone
      c. Social zone
      d. Public zone
    4. Time
    5. Voice and paralanguage
  E. Using Nonverbal Symbols to Establish Your Image
    1. Level of confidence
      a. Too much confidence
      b. Too little confidence
    2. Friendliness
    3. Enthusiasm
    4. Sincerity
    5. Appearance (Use Transparency 3-3 here.)
    6. Body actions
      a. Eye contact
      b. Posture

F. Nonverbal Symbols in the Environment
    1. Furnishings
    2. Color
II. Listening: An Important Interpersonal Skill
    A. The Importance of Listening
        1. The listening process (Use Transparency 3-4 here to help illustrate the listening process.)
            a. Hearing
            b. Focusing attention
            c. Understanding
            d. Remembering
        2. Types of listening
            a. Casual listening
            b. Active listening
        3. Reasons for listening
        4. Benefits of listening
    B. The Nature of Listening
        1. Barriers to effective listening
            a. Attitudes about the speaker
            b. Attitudes about the topic
            c. Environmental distractions
            d. Personal barriers
            e. Note-taking techniques
    C. Effective Listening Techniques
        1. Share the responsibility
            a. Focus on the main idea
            b. Evaluate the message
            c. Provide feedback
    D. Overcome Poor Listening Habits
    E. Listening in Specific Situations
        1. Listening in a small group. This is an extremely important place to listen—you demonstrate if you are ready for more responsibility.
        2. Listening in a conference setting. This is another important place to demonstrate effective listening skills. Ask students what would happen if they were sent to a conference and came back without the needed information.

Classroom Strategies

Emphasize to students that interpreting nonverbal symbols and listening effectively (which includes interpreting nonverbal symbols) are key skills for effective communicators—both senders and receivers. An individual who does not understand the nonverbal symbols sent with a message or who does not listen effectively will not move up in an organization.

The activities connected with these two sections need to be experiential. Thus, using the activities at the end of the chapter is key in helping students understand the importance of these two aspects of communication.

To experience the importance of nonverbal communication, have students complete Exercise 1 in the *Study Guide*. To improve their listening skills, have them complete Exercises 4 and 5 in the *Study Guide*.

Solutions to End-of-Section Activities

Discussion Questions

Section 3.1

1. Nonverbal communication is very important. These symbols provide additional information and help in interpreting and understanding verbal messages.
2. Yes. In both types of messages, receivers use nonverbal symbols to identify the sender's attitudes and feelings about the message and the receiver.
3. The nonverbal symbols that help to establish a credible personal image are level of confidence, friendliness, enthusiasm, sincerity, appearance, and body actions (eye contact, facial expressions, gestures, and posture).

Section 3.2

1. Yes, listening is important. We use it to relax, obtain information, express interest, and discover attitudes. Listening (a) improves the quality of relationships; (b) helps people better understand their own feelings, attitudes, and beliefs as well as those of others; (c) helps employees feel a part of the group; (d) improves the quality of decisions; and (e) contributes to success in business.
2. Listening is difficult because it requires remembering. To remember, you must hear, focus, and understand. These three parts of listening require self-discipline and concentration. Sometimes exercising self-discipline and concentrating is difficult.

3. The four major activities of effective listeners are to share the responsibility for communication, focus on the main idea of the speaker, evaluate the message, and provide feedback. Ten specific things we can do are
   a. find common interests
   b. judge content, not delivery
   c. delay judgment until the speaker is finished
   d. listen for the main idea
   e. take notes on only the important points
   f. concentrate on listening—stay alert
   g. avoid physical and environmental distractions
   h. listen with an open mind—do not let prejudices or assumptions cause you to miss the message
   i. use your spare time to analyze and review the message
   j. talk less—listen more

Solutions to End-of-Chapter Activities

Critical Thinking Questions

1. Nonverbal symbols are used to help understand a message. Remembering is the last step in the listening process. Thus, nonverbal symbols help us listen effectively.
2. They are equally important. To aid understanding, nonverbal symbols and listening are interdependent.

Applications

Part A
1. d
2. e
3. b
4. a
5. c
6. f

Part B
1. d
2. c
3. c
4. c
5. b

Part C. Students' answers will vary. Example answer:

Today, I visited the Department of Computer Information Systems. The office is very neat and tidy. Chairs are in place and clean. They are also tastefully upholstered to complement the pictures on the walls, the color of the walls, and the carpet. The pictures on the wall are masculine—pictures of ducks in the wild—but attractive. The desks, though people were working, looked organized. In summary, it is an office in which I could work and be happy.

Part D. Students' answers will vary. Example answer:

The Sony web page is very attractive. It uses color, pictures, and moving boxes to advertise its products—music, movies, television programs, and electronic products. Also, it advertises its TV games by letting you play the games (Jeopardy and Wheel of Fortune) online. If you click on the moving boxes, it takes you to that area for further detail.

Part E. Students' answers will vary. Example answer:

I was able to converse for (*time*) minutes because I picked a topic my friend is interested in. Casual listening is easier than active listening because our subject was social rather than academic.

Part F. Students' answers will vary. Example answer:

I would rate my listener as average. He exhibited boredom when pretending to listen to his teacher. He also seemed to let his mind wander. However, he did take notes and did try to listen for the main ideas. (I saw his notes, and they were somewhat organized.) He even asked a question when he wasn't sure about the meaning of part of the teacher's presentation.

Editing Activities

Corrected words or phrases are underlined.

1. If you take a computer course at a college or university, you might be eligible for an account on its computer system. This is a great way to get to the Internet because most reasonably large colleges and universities have Internet connections. You might have to use one of their computers, or you might be able to dial in from home using your own computer and modem.

2. Freenets are, as <u>their</u> name implies, free! If you are lucky enough to have one in <u>your</u> area, you have hit the jackpot. To find out if there is a Freenet in your locality, check with <u>computer</u> stores, user groups, and the Chamber of <u>Commerce</u>. The <u>problems</u> with Freenets <u>are</u> that there are not many of them, they can be erratic in the service they provide, they often come and go <u>without</u> notice, and logging on is often difficult because of a lack of phone lines.

Case Studies

1. **To the Instructor:** Tell the students you are going to have a role-playing activity. Ask them to read the "Situation" as it is described in the text. Select four students for the roles to be played—a manager, an assistant manager, and two applicants. Copy the roles and the lists of questions, if necessary, and give them to the appropriate students. After giving the applicants their roles, tell them to leave the room and wait to be called in for an interview. Give the appropriate roles and lists of questions to the manager and assistant manager.

   List of Questions for Manager: (1) I see you are attending a local college. Why are you going to school? (2) Are you taking any classes that would help you with this position? (3) With regards to this position, what is the greatest strength you have to offer? (4) With regards to this position, what is the greatest weakness you have? (5) We have had several strong applicants for this position. Why should we hire you?

   Role of the Manager: As the manager, you are very business-oriented and personable. Ask the questions with a normal relaxed tone. If you ask follow-up questions to a response of an applicant, try to ask the next candidate the same follow-up questions.

   List of Questions for the Assistant Manager: (1) Are you married and do you have children? (2) Do you attend church on Sunday and if so, where? (This is an illegal question to ask.) (3) What experience do you have that would help you with this position?

   Role of the Assistant Manager: The assistant manager is also very business-oriented. However, this person is not very personable. Thus, when asking questions, this individual asks them in a very sharp, quick tone. Do not ask any follow-up questions.

   Role of Applicant 1: This applicant is somewhat shy. You answer questions in a very soft tone of voice and do not give any additional information besides the needed information to answer each question. For example, when asked, "What experience do you have that would help you with this position?" the response could be, "I worked at Burger King on Lance Avenue for one year."

   Role of Applicant 2: This applicant is very talkative but seems distracted during the interview. Make your answers long even if they ramble. To appear distracted, after the manager or assistant manager has asked one or two of his or her questions, respond by saying, "What? Would you repeat the question again?"

   Students' answers to the last instruction will vary. However, the memorandums should be written in a simplified memorandum format.

2. Students' answers will vary. Example answer:
   a. I would tell him the truth—you are a poor listener.
   b. Yes, nonverbal communication would play a role. Hopefully, my nonverbal communication would tell him that I am sincere and not trying to be negative. I would try to tell him in a humble, sincere manner.
   c. The suggestions should be the same as those given in the answer to Discussion Question 3 in Section 3.2. The web site provides information that would lead to the following suggestions: (1) go to work rested, (2) ask questions to clarify, (3) nod and give visual evidence of interest, (4) ask for feedback on what you do, and (5) show awareness of the importance of listening by sharing listening techniques with others.

Career Case Studies

Communication for Business and Marketing Careers

1. Listening will be very important in Mr. Ridingbull's business. First, hosts and servers must listen to customers as they come into the restaurant and as they place their orders. Customers must listen to the servers as they explain the menu or provide other pieces of information that will be helpful to them. Then, if not done electronically, chefs must listen to the servers as orders are placed. At the end of a meal, customers will need to listen to the servers

so that the meals can be paid for; servers will have to listen to customers to accommodate them in the payment of their bills.

2. Nonverbal communication will also be very important. Besides the architectural design of the restaurant, furnishings and color should be used to set an appropriate atmosphere for the restaurant. Tables, chairs, server uniforms, dress attire for hosts, and dress attire for chefs all will be important elements of the nonverbal communication symbols used in the restaurant.

Communication for Human and Social Services Careers

1. Julius should wear at least slacks, a white shirt, and a tie.
2. Julius should try to project a professional image. Key elements of that image are self-confidence, friendliness, enthusiasm, sincerity, good grooming, appropriate dress, good eye contact, and good posture.
3. Julius should expect both types of listening. Julius will be expected to remember and know some material—requiring active listening. He will not be expected to know and remember other material—requiring casual listening.
4. He can ensure his understanding of the messages sent to him by paraphrasing the messages.
5. He can demonstrate that he understands the messages of the agencies by paraphrasing the messages.
6. Probably. He should first ask the attendant of the booth if he or she minds if he takes notes. If note-taking is acceptable, then he should take notes so that he can remember who said what. If the attendant indicates that he or she prefers no notes, then he should not take them. However, in most cases, they will probably allow note-taking.

Video Case

1. Students could write that listening is crucial for discovering a patient's condition or what may have led up to that condition. Listening reassures a patient that someone is trying to help. Listening to family and friends of the patient suggests ways they can be reassured. Listening to a fellow ambulance crew member might help

that person deal with a difficult call. Similarly, students might cite several examples of nonverbal skills affecting the crew/patient relation such as a paramedic bending down to listen to an elderly woman sitting on a sofa or a paramedic looking someone in the face as she describes the condition of an injured friend. The video also shows examples of ambulance crew members talking calmly to a patient.

2. There may be some overlap in the characterizations named by people interviewed, so the number of characteristics doesn't matter. In fact, it might be valuable for students to see that the traits of a good listener keep reappearing in the interviews. Students might have to explain what nonverbal communication is to interviewees.
3. Students can draw on the benefits shown in the video (benefiting both the patient and the ambulance crew member) or refer to the information in the chapter. For example, the video shows the importance of listening in understanding others and making good decisions. Students might also describe listening as crucial to the high-stress customer service the ambulance crews dispense.

Continuing Case

1. Yes, Eva misread it. Isako may be avoiding eye contact to show that she respects Eva as her teacher. Avoiding eye contact is a sign of respect in many Asian cultures.
2. By looking directly at Kevin, Eva implies that she is interested only in his questions.
3. Students' answers may vary. Verbally, Eva encouraged student questions and answered them. She expressed an interest in whether Kevin had a computer at home, and she urged Clara and Kevin to return. However, Eva's nonverbal messages included not encouraging questions from Isako and Clara, interrupting Clara, and not listening to Kevin as he started to answer her question about his computer. Students may believe that Eva's actions spoke louder than her words.
4. Students' e-mail messages should recommend that Eva not make assumptions about her students, pay attention to all of them equally, and try not to interrupt anyone.

Chapter 4 The Writing Process

Student Learning Objectives

Section 1
- Understand the prewriting stage of the writing process.
- Plan messages by identifying the objective and main idea.
- Choose supporting information in messages.
- Adjust messages for the receiver and write receiver-oriented messages.
- Organize messages.

Section 2
- Use prewriting notes to create a draft.
- Write courteous messages.
- Create a positive tone.
- Choose bias-free language.
- Choose precise and concise words.

Section 3
- Revise a draft to improve organization and flow.
- Write concise sentences.
- Eliminate unnecessary sentence elements.
- Describe the sentence and paragraph structure of business messages.
- Include the five *W*s (*who, what, where, when,* and *why*) in messages.
- Vary sentence style and paragraph length.
- Use transitions to connect sentences and paragraphs.

Section 4
- Edit your own business communications for clarity, completeness, and tone.
- Proofread for content and mechanical errors.
- Use different methods of proofreading.
- Use proofreaders' marks.

Section 5
- Generate error-free, attractive business communications.

- Format documents appropriately.
- Incorporate graphics to enhance a business message.

Teaching Outline

Introductory Points
- Understanding the fundamentals of business writing helps writers create a better product.
- Planning carefully and thoughtfully enables business writers to produce correspondence that will be accepted by readers.
- Using the writing process aids writers in carrying out the necessary planning, organizing, and refining of a document.
- The basic structure of sentences and paragraphs contributes to the tone of a message and how it is received by the reader.
- Producing error-free messages by editing and proofreading carefully is vital. (Use Transparency 4-1.)

I. Prewriting: Planning and Organizing Messages
   A. The Writing Process
      1. The stages of the writing process include prewriting, drafting, revising, editing and proofreading, and publishing.
      2. During prewriting, writers plan, conduct research, and gather information.
      3. Writers should focus on purpose, audience, length, and medium during the prewriting stage.
   B. Planning Business Messages
      1. Writers must identify which of the four objectives—in addition to promoting goodwill—they hope to accomplish in each business message they write. (Use Transparency 4-2.)
         a. To inform
         b. To request
         c. To record
         d. To persuade
      2. Writers must then identify the main idea of a message.
      3. To reinforce the main idea, the writer includes supporting information, such as facts, examples, or reasons.

4. Writers must write considerate messages with content that is appropriate for their receivers. (Use Transparency 4-3.)
C. Organizing Messages
   1. Direct order—main idea followed by supporting details—is best for positive or neutral messages.
   2. Indirect order—supporting details followed by main idea—is usually used for negative messages.
   3. Direct-indirect order—positive main idea and supporting information followed by negative supporting information and main idea—is used when a message is both positive and negative. (Use Transparency 4-4.)

II. Drafting: Choosing Words
  A. Drafting
   1. Writers use prewriting notes or organizational tools to shape their ideas into sentences and paragraphs.
   2. Writers focus on ideas, not on details such as spelling or grammar.
  B. Courteous Words
   1. Use positive words, even in a negative message, to make your message more courteous and less unpleasant.
   2. Use proper titles, such as *Mr.*, *Ms.*, and *Dr.*, to show respect to receivers.
   3. Avoid words that show bias in terms of gender, race, age, or ability.
  C. Appropriate Words
   1. Precise words are vivid and informative.
   2. Concise words carry complete meaning but do not include redundancies.

III. Revising: Creating Concise Sentences and Complete Paragraphs
  A. Revising
   1. During the revising stage, consider the overall logic, tone, and structure of a message.
   2. Focus on paragraph and sentence structure and flow.
  B. Concise Sentences
   1. Do not include unnecessary elements, redundancies, empty phrases, or wordiness in sentences.
   2. Concise writers write in the active voice rather than in the passive voice.

C. Complete Paragraphs
   1. Sentences in a paragraph focus on one thought or idea.
   2. Most paragraphs contain a beginning, or topic, sentence; one or more middle sentences that develop the topic; and an ending sentence that closes the paragraph.
   3. Complete business messages contain an opening paragraph, at least one developmental paragraph, and a closing paragraph.
   4. Complete paragraphs include all necessary information. (Use Transparency 4-5.)
   5. Varying sentence structure and length makes a message more interesting and easier to understand.
D. Clear Paragraphs
   1. A clear paragraph has unity—it expresses one idea.
   2. Transition words and phrases show relationships between thoughts and ideas and help readers move from one sentence to the next.

IV. Editing and Proofreading
  A. Editing
   1. To edit is to alter or refine a written message to improve it.
   2. When editing, concentrate on the accuracy and effectiveness of sentences, phrases, and words.
   3. Consider the clarity, completeness, and tone of a business message during editing.
  B. Proofreading
   1. Proofreading is the process of reviewing and correcting the final draft of a written message.
   2. Proofreaders should look first for general content errors, then for mechanical errors such as misspelled words, incorrect punctuation, and so on.
   3. Proofreading methods include scrolling the screen, reading aloud, comparing drafts, proofreading hard copy, proofreading backwards, and using two proofreaders.

4. Word processing software has spell checkers and grammar checkers, but writers must still proofread their work carefully for errors that a computer cannot detect.
5. Use standard proofreaders' marks to note corrections on your own and others' drafts.

V. Publishing
  A. Finalizing Your Message
     1. To publish is to deliver a message to the receiver, or to make the message available to the public.
     2. Final documents must be error-free.
     3. A final document should be printed on high-quality paper with dark ink.
     4. The margins of a document should allow an appropriate amount of white space around the edges of the page.
     5. Writers should use fonts and font sizes that are appropriate for business communications.
     6. Setting headings in a boldface sans serif font and text in a serif font makes a document easy for receivers to read.
  B. Enhancing Your Message
     1. Well-chosen and well-rendered graphics can add information or summarize complex information in a business message.
     2. Graphics should be numbered consecutively and titled or captioned in a consistent manner.
     3. If a writer borrows ideas or acquires data from another source, that source must be cited immediately below a graphic.

Classroom Strategies

The concept of a writing *process* is likely not new to students. Help them see that they use the process without even realizing it for everyday or informal correspondence connected with school and current jobs. Emphasize that consciously following the steps for more formal or longer business messages will help them develop good habits when it comes to acquiring information, organizing information, and perfecting the presentation of that information.

Share with students examples of nonconfidential e-mail, memos, or letters you receive as part of your job. Have students evaluate the correspondence at several levels throughout their study of the chapter. Alternately, students may share their own examples of nonconfidential and nonpersonal correspondence. Make sure students can distinguish good examples from bad. Have them consider the planning and organizing that went into examples they evaluate.

The case studies at the end of the chapter give a great deal of background information so that students can understand the complexities of the situations. You may wish to discuss the scenarios before students complete the associated writing assignments. Or, you may have students provide a written evaluation of the situation along with the suggested assignment. Point out that when students are in their own work environments, they must be aware of the complexities of their own situations in terms of coworkers' personalities, office procedures, and office "politics."

Solutions to End-of-Section Activities

Discussion Questions

Section 4.1

1. Writers can use the prewriting stage to plan, collect information, and organize their thoughts and ideas by using outlines, charts, or diagrams. When they draft, they can use their organizational tools to transform their ideas from note form to sentences and paragraphs. If something doesn't work, they can go back to the prewriting stage to pursue new ideas or try a new method of organization.
2. Receivers accept the content of a business message more readily if the message contains some goodwill.
3. The message may be incomplete or disorganized, which may cause confusion for the receiver or may mislead the receiver in some way. The result may be that the receiver rejects the message, or responds in a way that the writer did not intend.
4. Make sure students can distinguish between the message's objective and its main idea. Students should be able to map out the message's organization and conclude that it is direct, indirect, or direct-indirect. Evaluations will vary.

Section 4.2

1. When drafting, a writer should concentrate on getting ideas down on paper in some kind of logical order. It's called a rough draft because it may contain errors in organization, word choice, spelling, grammar, and so on.
2. A message with a positive tone is more reader-friendly than a message that lacks a positive tone. Even if a writer must send a negative message, a positive tone, combined with a you-attitude, help ensure that the receiver will *accept* the message.
3. Titles are a sign of respect. Showing respect is part of being courteous. Avoiding bias in business communications is vital in today's culturally diverse workplace. If a message contains bias, certain readers may be offended or may simply disregard the message.
4. Redundant expressions are empty or wordy phrases that seem formal but lack meaning. Business writing should be concise and straightforward, not full of empty or flowery language.

Section 4.3

1. Most businesspeople receive many communications each day. Concisely written messages will get the readers' attention because they are easy to read and their message is easy to grasp.
2. I can use active voice, avoid empty or wordy phrases, and use concrete language that conveys exactly what I mean and tells the receiver exactly what he or she needs to know.
3. The receivers may be confused or misled. Also, sending an incomplete message makes the writer appear careless or unskilled.
4. A business message must tell receivers everything they need to know. What they need to know is usually covered by the five *W*s—*who, what, where, when,* and *why.*
5. Students may suggest that they can go through the five *W*s themselves to make sure they have included all information receivers might need. A quick read-through specifically to check sentence length can inform students about their sentence variety.

Section 4.4

1. Business communications must express their messages clearly and be free of errors. The process of editing and proofreading ensures that communications are effective and correct in terms of content and form or mechanics.

2. On the first pass, look for general content errors, such as missing or repeated words, transposed words, incorrect names, or incorrect use of a word. On the second pass, look for mechanical errors, including incorrect spacing, misspellings, missing punctuation, and incorrect capitalization. Proofreaders are less likely to miss errors if they look for one kind of error at a time.
3. Answers will vary.

Section 4.5

1. During the publishing step, writers create an error-free final document.
2. Readers have expectations about what printed materials look like. They expect printed documents to conform to certain standards, and they expect them to be reasonably easy to read. A document that is disorganized looking or crowded will not invite readers to read.
3. They might assume the writer is incompetent or unprofessional or that he or she has a poor attitude about the message or the receiver.
4. Answers will vary.

Solutions to End-of-Chapter Activities

Critical Thinking Questions

1. Students should list and describe the five steps: prewriting, drafting, revising, editing and proofreading, and publishing. Students' comments on their use of the process should demonstrate some self-awareness of their writing skills.
2. Business messages may be written to promote goodwill, to inform, to request, to record, or to persuade. Students' examples will vary.
3. If the receiver can't understand a message because it's too complicated, or is offended by a message because it is too simplistic, the sender has not communicated effectively. To write effectively, the sender must communicate at the level of the receiver's comprehension. If the sender does not write *for* the receiver, all other issues of organization, word choice, structure, and so on, are invalid.
4. Receivers are more willing to accept the content of a polite, positive message than they are the content of one that does not contain courtesy or

signs of respect. Writers can maintain a positive tone by being professional, by being respectful, and by keeping in mind the receiver's point of view. If a message is negative, don't blurt it out in the first line. Express goodwill and make statements to prepare the receiver for the negative message.

5. A proofreader's eye may see what it *thinks* is there, rather than what is actually there. Reading aloud or backward forces the proofreader to see each letter and word and punctuation mark.

Applications

Part A. Answers will vary. Students' letters should be receiver-oriented. Look for complete information about claiming the prize.

Part B. Answers will vary. The tone of the message should be positive and should promote goodwill, in spite of the negative message. Letters should be organized in indirect order.

Part C. Answers will vary. (1) The e-mail message should include a suggested meeting time, date, and place, as well as a brief explanation of the purpose of the meeting. The explanation should contain no bias. (2) This message should be a summary. It should not represent either of the writer's coworkers in a negative light, even if one or both of them didn't like the boss's idea.

Editing Activities

Part A. Answers will vary. A sample solution follows.

Electronically prepared letters are a common part of today's society. In fact, they provide a major challenge for communicators who strive to make these communications successful. Fortunately, the skills needed to prepare electronic letters are the same as those needed to prepare traditional communications.

Part B. Answers will vary. A sample solution follows.

Welcome to Atten Mortgage Company. A brochure is enclosed. It contains the answers to many questions you may have about your new mortgage loan. Mortgage payment coupons, which must accompany all payments, will be mailed separately. Your loan number is located in the upper left corner of each payment coupon.

Case Studies

1. Answers will vary. Students should suggest that Steve include photos of an already completed playhouse at his site. Also, his description of possible playhouse designs could be specific without being technical. He should represent his skills more professionally, rather than just as a hobby.

2. Answers will vary. Students' letters should begin by promoting goodwill—praising the employee for good work, loyalty, extra hours put in to meet deadlines, and so on. The letter should acknowledge the disadvantages of having to hire employees temporarily. Termination details should include the employee's last day of work, any payment arrangements, and any final responsibilities, such as turning in a key. The final statement should be a further expression of goodwill.

Career Case Studies

Communication for Human and Social Services Careers

1. Answers will vary. The tone of the letter to the Mallorys is very important. It must express concern, not complaint. It must speak to the parents as partners of the teacher in Austin's development. It must not send the message that the parents are causing the problem, nor that they are alone in having to "fix" the problem. Promoting goodwill is a given in this letter, since the Mallorys are Tina's customers. It is probably best if the letter goes beyond just informing the parents; it should ask for their support in changing the child's behavior.

2. Writers may list specific goals for the child and suggest how the parents and teachers, working together, may help Austin achieve those goals.

Communication for Health Services Careers

1. Answers will vary. Malcolm's e-mail, like all e-mail, should be relatively brief. Because he is writing to his supervisor, he needs to show appropriate respect for her and for the hospital's normal procedures when it comes to disseminating information to employees. The message must inform without complaining.

2. It may or may not suggest a course of action, such as a staff meeting or a memo issued from the supervisor.

Continuing Case

1. No. It does not have a you-attitude. It talks about what the shop offers but says little about how these services will benefit the customers. Also, the intended readers do not need to know about the shop's three target groups of customers.

2. "You may not have heard of us . . . "; "you have never seen . . . "; "you will not find . . . "; "small but fair fee"; negative comment about the "elderly"; negative description of group 3; "can't afford to offer free computer services. . . ."

3. Possibly the silent partners or other potential investors.

4. who (letter should be signed with names of partners), where (shop address), when (hours), why (more about why customers should visit the shop)

5. third paragraph: *if/of*; group 1: *out/our*; last paragraph: *thin/this*

6. Students' revised letters should delete the description of the three target groups, have a positive tone, and avoid age or other biases. Their letters should be you-oriented, stressing benefits that customers can receive by visiting the NetCafe, such as learning more about computers in a relaxed setting, using the shop's up-to-date equipment and software applications for special projects and presentations, using e-mail, and enjoying their favorite coffee in a friendly atmosphere.

Chapter 5
Writing Memos, E-mail, and Other Communications

Student Learning Objectives

Section 1
- Explain how memos are used in internal communication.
- Explain how electronic memos, e-mail messages, are used in internal communication.
- Describe when to use memos and e-mail messages.

Section 2
- Identify the parts of a memo.
- Understand traditional and simplified memo formats.
- Explain ways to organize memos and e-mail messages.
- List and explain the guidelines for writing effective memos and e-mail messages.

Section 3
- Identify and describe the abuses of memos and e-mail messages.
- Understand possible remedies for abuses.
- Identify some common abuses particular to e-mail messages.

Section 4
- Describe several kinds of meetings.
- Develop and write meeting agendas.
- Draft minutes to report meeting results.
- Write a mission statement and a vision statement for a business.

Teaching Outline

Introductory Points
- The memo has traditionally been the most common internal document due to its speed and informality; however, e-mail is quickly replacing the hard-copy memo because of its many advantages.
- Formatting of memos and e-mails is becoming less of an issue with the advent of memo forms, word processors, wizards, templates, and e-mail software.
- Avoiding the abuses and misuses of memos and e-mail will gain respect and credibility for the writer.
- Knowing how to organize and write meeting agendas and minutes may seem outdated, but it is a precise and appreciated skill.

I. Uses of Internal Documents
  A. Internal Documents
    1. Memos are the most common internal business communication. (Use Transparency 5-1.)
    2. E-mails are quickly replacing the hard-copy memo.
  B. Business Memos
    1. Memos are usually less formal, quicker, and easier than letters.
    2. Memos can be sent via hard copy or electronically.
    3. More and more companies and individuals are using e-mail.
  C. E-mail Messages
    1. Telecommuting is a growing way to conduct business.
    2. There are many advantages to using e-mail.
      a. Messages can be sent to several people simultaneously.
      b. E-mail can be sent readily to anyone listed in your address book, the feature that stores frequently used e-mail addresses.
      c. Messages are sent in real time—information is exchanged instantaneously.
      d. Multiple messages can be sent with just a few keystrokes.
      e. E-mail can be sent globally instantly.
      f. Messages can be sent day or night, whether or not the receiver is available. The message is held in an electronic mailbox, the computer storage file that holds the e-mail until the receiver opens the system and reads the mail.

g. E-mail can be sent or received on both networked and stand-alone computers equipped with modems (transmitters of electronic signals via telephone lines).

h. Documents from other software programs (such as a spreadsheet) can be attached to the e-mail message.

i. Whether long or short, documents can be transmitted in seconds.

j. E-mail memos may convey a sense of urgency and importance that hard-copy memos or letters don't.

k. Internal e-mail systems are relatively inexpensive.

D. Memos—When to Use Them

1. Memos and e-mails are usually less time-consuming; can be sent to more than one receiver; and are less expensive than letters, conference calls, etc.

2. Memos and e-mails are used to provide a record; advise, direct, or state policy; inform; and promote goodwill.

II. Formatting and Writing Effective Internal Documents

A. Parts of a Memo

1. The standard parts of a memo are the heading, the body, and the notations.

2. The components of the heading are TO, FROM, DATE, and SUBJECT.

B. Formatting Memos

1. If you are not using a template or wizard, follow one of the two memo styles: traditional or simplified.

2. Traditional style is often used with letterhead stationery. (Use Transparency 5-2.)

3. The simplified format is often used on word processors or on forms. (Use Transparency 5-3.)

C. Guidelines for Planning and Organizing Memos and E-mail Messages

1. To plan a memo or e-mail, identify the objective, identify the main idea, determine the supporting information, and adjust the content to the receiver. (Use Transparency 5-4.)

2. Use the direct order for good news and the indirect order for bad news or persuasion.

3. The indirect order is made of three parts: a neutral beginning, supporting information, and the main idea.

D. Guidelines for Writing Memos and E-mail Messages

1. After the planning and organizing stages, come the writing and editing tasks.

2. There are seven guidelines to help with memo and e-mail writing and editing. (Use Transparency 5-5.)

a. Restrict a memo to one main idea.

b. Compose a short, clear subject line.

c. Make the body stand alone.

d. Use tables and visual aids.

e. Use headings in long memos.

f. Number or bullet items in a list.

g. Proofread your message.

III. Abuses of Internal Documents

A. When Not to Use Memos and E-mail Messages

1. Do not write memos and e-mails too frequently or the result may be communication overload.

2. Do not write to gain attention or to brag.

3. Do not write these messages by committee.

4. Do not send the same message to different audiences—tailor it to fit your receiver.

B. Common E-mail Abuses

1. Some abuses are particular to e-mail.

2. Avoid these eight e-mail abuses.

a. Do not send mass, unsolicited messages, called spamming.

b. Do not ramble on and on or change subjects.

c. Do not write in one continuous paragraph.

d. Do not write an offensive message.

e. Do not use all caps, called shouting.

f. Do make sloppy errors because of the immediacy of e-mail.

g. Do not overuse emoticons.

h. Do not send angry or insulting anonymous messages, called flaming.

i. Do not send chain letter e-mail messages.

IV. Meetings and Other Internal Communications
  A. Meetings
    1. There are many kinds of meetings, such as board, training, staff, committee, and conferences.
    2. Committees may be standing, ad hoc, or a task force.
  B. Meeting Notices
    1. Notices are usually delivered by memo or e-mail.
    2. Notices should include date, time, location, and possibly an agenda.
  C. Agendas
    1. An agenda should include the order of business to be discussed at the meeting.
    2. To plan an agenda, determine the meeting objectives and topics. (Use Transparency 5-6.)
    3. Agendas may or may not include the call to order, the roll call, approval of minutes from the previous meeting, old business, new business, announcements, and adjournment.
  D. Minutes
    1. The minutes are the official record of a meeting.
    2. A copy of the minutes may be given to attendees, those who were absent, and those who need to know the information covered.
  E. Mission and Vision Statements
    1. A mission statement describes a business's purpose.
    2. A vision statement indicates what a business is striving to become.

Classroom Strategies

Explain that the ability to plan, format, and write clear, concise memos and e-mail messages is vital in both the business and personal environments of today. Use the chapter to acquaint students with memos as internal communications and to differentiate between the traditional and the simplified memo formats.

Draw on students' experiences with various communications to discuss the direct and indirect orders and their validity. Their experiences may also provide a discussion base for the abuses and misuses of memos and e-mail. You and your students might bring to class written examples of effective and ineffective memos and e-mails.

Finally, introduce the various kinds of business meetings and present guidelines for writing agendas and minutes. Use this chapter to remind students of the diversity of documents they will prepare during the course of their careers. Finally, while absorbing this chapter, students need to realize that the appearance and content of a document reflect the professionalism of the writer.

Solutions to End-of-Section Activities

Discussion Questions

Section 5.1

1. Memos are a quick and easy way to communicate in writing with a colleague or a supervisor in the same department, in another department, or in another company office.
2. The advantages of an e-mail message over a hard-copy memo are:
   - Messages can be sent to several people simultaneously.
   - E-mail can be sent readily to anyone listed in your address book, the feature that stores frequently used e-mail addresses.
   - Messages are sent in real time—information is exchanged instantaneously.
   - Multiple messages can be sent with just a few keystrokes.
   - E-mail can be sent globally, around the world, instantly.
   - Messages can be sent day or night, whether the receiver is available or not. The message is held in an electronic mailbox, the computer storage file that holds the e-mail until the receiver opens the system and reads the mail.
   - E-mail can be sent or received on both networked and stand-alone computers equipped with modems (transmitters of electronic signals via telephone lines).
   - Documents from other software programs (such as a spreadsheet) can be attached to the e-mail message.
   - Whether long or short, documents can be transmitted in seconds.

- E-mail memos may convey a sense of urgency and importance that hard-copy memos or letters don't.
- Internal e-mail systems are relatively inexpensive.

Section 5.2

1. In the traditional memo format, the heading appears at the top of the page. In contrast, the simplified memo format does not include a heading. The simplified memo is more easily produced in a template or on a computer or word processor.

2. The guidelines students may cite are to (1) restrict a memo to one main idea, (2) compose a short, clear subject line, (3) make the body stand alone, (4) use tables and visual aids, (5) use headings in long memos, and (6) number or bullet items in a list.

3. Answers will vary, but students should give examples to support their choices, such as "Lists should be bulleted to ease eye strain for the reader."

Section 5.3

1. Students may disagree about when it is *not* appropriate to send a memo, but their discussion should consider when a more formal letter may be better (congratulations, condolences, formal policies) and the needs of the receiver (for privacy, formality, and so forth).

2. Common abuses of memos are that they are (1) written too frequently, (2) written to gain attention, (3) written by committee, and (4) rewritten for each level of management.

3. Answers will vary. Students should realize that proper e-mail etiquette will help keep the channels open in effective communication.

Section 5.4

1. The purpose of an agenda is to provide a written guide and order of business for a particular meeting. If it is distributed in advance, an agenda helps the attendees prepare for the meeting.

2. The discussion may revolve around these ideas: Minutes are important to keep as an official (and sometimes legal) record of the proceedings of a meeting; they may summarize important points for later review; and they may provide a record for people who could not attend.

3. Mission and vision statements are important because they focus a business's employees on its purpose and what it wants to become.

Solutions to End-of-Chapter Activities

Critical Thinking Questions

1. Students may disagree on the uses of memos versus e-mail messages. They may say that a hard-copy memo can be better posted, passed around a distribution list, and filed. If someone hands out a memo, there is certainty that it has been received. Also, people who are not comfortable with computers would need a hard-copy memo.

2. More and more, people who use computers are using e-mail as their preferred mode of transmitting messages. Students may cite some of the reasons given in the key to Discussion Question 2 in Section 5.1. They may point out that an e-mail can always be printed out and, therefore, become a hard-copy memo.

3. The language used in a memo to a colleague might well be more informal or personal than the language to a client. It might also include insider terms, technical vocabulary, abbreviations, or acronyms that only a colleague would understand.

4. Students may mention that the following should not be included in the minutes: private comments, high-security issues, swearing, and irrelevant comments.

Applications

Part A
1. Main idea = celebration of promotion; use = to promote goodwill and to inform.
2. Main idea = recommendation to open a new branch in Lancaster; use = to inform or provide a record.
3. Main idea = statement of the annual vacation leave policy; use = to advise, direct, and state policy and to inform.

Part B. Use Transparency 5-7. Assign a specific purpose for the memo written by each group: (1) to state policy, (2) to state policy and to maintain or promote goodwill, and (3) to provide a record to show that the memo was written as instructed by your supervisor. Each group is not to know the purpose assigned to other groups.

Part C. The only misspelled word is "minites" and should be *minutes*. An agenda prepared from the memo might look like this:

Agenda
Cool-Touch Toaster, New-Product Promotion Meeting
Thursday, January 19, 20—
2:00 p.m.
Conference Room B

1. Call to Order
2. Roll Call
3. Review and Approval of the December Meeting's Minutes
4. Chairpersons' Reports
   A. Advertising Subcommittee
   B. In-store Promotions Subcommittee
5. Chairperson's Report
   A. Production Schedule
   B. Sample of New Packaging
6. Unfinished Business
   A. Warranty Period
   B. Sales Incentives
7. New Business
   A. New Product Ideas
   B. Other New Business
8. Announcements
9. Adjournment

Part D. Answers will vary but should consist of two e-mails that use e-mail etiquette.

Editing Activities

I. Words correctly spelled: medical, patient's, system, supervisor, extension, department.

II. Answers will vary. Example: This is not a good memo. The writer is trying to gain the supervisor's attention with unnecessary flattery and gratitude. Also, the mention of what the writer can afford is inappropriate. The writer has abused the use of a memo.

Case Studies

1. Student memos will vary. Check to see that they have used the indirect order and positive language to write this memo in the simplified memo format. You might discuss how such a bad-news memo can be diplomatic and honest, without being euphemistic. Share the best examples with the class.
2. Student e-mails will vary. Share the best/worst examples and ask students to compare them

and to comment on their effectiveness. You might also discuss how writing to subordinates may or may not be different than writing to other receivers.

Career Case Studies

Communication for Natural Resources and Agriculture Careers

1. Answers will vary, but a possible main idea for Laura's memo is "What has changed at Arrow Lake in the last week to kill the fish?"
2. Some samples of questions Laura might ask her wildlife rangers are:
   - At what part of the lake have you seen the dead fish?
   - Have you observed any unusual substances, either excess vegetation or foreign materials, in the lake?
   - Have you found any other dead wildlife?
   - Do you have any theories as to what is happening?
   - What have our lake water tests shown?
3. As for graphics, Laura might add a map of Arrow Lake with designated spots marked or an enlarged map of the dead-fish area. She might have charts of water testing results or a photograph of dead fish (since their appearance might elicit theories about what happened to them).

Communication for Engineering and Industrial Careers

Students' e-mails will vary. Check that they have employed the guidelines for both e-mail writing and bad-news communications. For example, the e-mail might begin with the good news that the installation of the rest of the subway system is ahead of schedule. You might share the better examples with the class and discuss why they are effective.

Video Case

1. Students can argue for a memo, letter, or e-mail. Those arguing for an e-mail might stress the urgency of Oscar's relaying information to the AEs and e-mail's built-in urgency. Those arguing against an e-mail might mention the guaranteed hard-copy form of a memo or letter or the deliberation required for such an important communication—not an e-mail's greatest strength. Those arguing for a letter might argue for its formality and the greater attention a letter can sometimes elicit. Those students might refer to the importance of Oscar's relaying important cultural

issues to the AEs. Students favoring a memo might mention that Oscar is writing an internal communication. These students might also mention the urgency of the situation and cite the lack of formatting and formal addresses required by a memo.

2. The video lists five areas of research and reasons for their importance:
   - Gifts—Make sure what is appropriate.
   - Greeting—Shake hands, kiss on one cheek or two, or bow, as appropriate.
   - Level of formality—Respect traditions of formality; some cultures have rules of formality thousands of years old.
   - Concept of time—Punctuality is very important in some cultures but may not be in others.
   - Holidays/traditions—Be sensitive; even the appearance of ignorance could kill a business relationship.

3. Students can augment the list by finding either additional areas or more examples of why the five areas are important. Answers will vary, but students will probably locate consulting companies that specialize in cross-cultural training.

Continuing Case

1. The subject is missing. It is important to include the topic of an e-mail in the subject line, so the recipient will quickly know what your message is about.

2. He uses the direct order. Students may note that he needs to use the more persuasive indirect order, since the company ignored his earlier reminder.

3. He should not use all capital letters or emoticons. Ramon should also break his e-mail into two or more paragraphs because he covers two topics.

4. The tone is angry and demanding. Ramon should have waited until he calmed down before sending this e-mail. He also should not have threatened the supplier at the end of his message.

5. No, because *desperate* is misspelled; this error would have been caught by a spell-checker. Ramon didn't read his e-mail carefully either, as shown in the substitutions *cane/can* and *Is/In* and the missing word *it* in the fifth sentence. A spell-checker would not catch these errors, but careful reading would.

6. Students' revised e-mails should be indirect, perhaps beginning with a positive comment about the Kenyan coffee. They should incorporate all the changes suggested or implied above. The request for the new blend of coffee should be omitted or discussed in its own paragraph. Students should then explain that their revised letters are more respectful and persuasive, which makes them more likely to convince the supplier to send the order.

7. Student answers will vary.

8. Student answers will vary.

Chapter 6 Writing Letters to Your Clients and Customers

Student Learning Objectives

Section 1
- Identify the use of letters.
- Select the correct order for letters.
- Describe the standard and optional parts of a business letter.
- Use the block, modified block, and simplified block formats.
- Prepare a business envelope.

Section 2
- Plan letters with neutral or positive messages.
- Organize letters with neutral or positive messages.
- Write letters with neutral or positive messages.

Section 3
- Plan letters containing negative messages.
- Organize letters containing negative messages.
- Write letters containing negative messages.

Teaching Outline

Introductory Points
- Letters are used as external documents.
- When written for a company, letters should be placed on letterhead.
- Letters are symbols representing your company and you.
- The appearance of a letter needs to be appealing to the receiver.

I. Selecting Order and Formatting Your Letters
  A. Use of Letters
  B. Identifying the Order of Your Letters
    1. Letters with a neutral or positive message employ the direct order.
    2. Letters with a negative message employ the indirect order.

  C. Letter Parts (Use Figure 6-1 to aid in the teaching of the parts of a letter.)
    1. Dateline
    2. Letter address
    3. Attention line
    4. Salutation
    5. Subject line
    6. Body
    7. Complimentary close
    8. Company name
    9. Signature block
    10. Reference initials
    11. Enclosure notation
    12. Copy notation
    13. Postscript
    14. Second-page heading (Use Transparency 6-3 to review the parts of a letter.)
  D. Business Letter Formats
    1. Placement on the page (Stress the importance of placement on a page. Use Transparencies 6-1 and 6-2 to illustrate the importance of placement.)
    2. Block format (Use Figure 6-2 to illustrate the block format with mixed punctuation.)
    3. Modified-block format (Use Transparency 6-4 for an illustration of a letter in the modified-block format. Point out the differences between the blocked and modified block formats.)
    4. Simplified block format (Use Transparency 6-5 for an example of a letter in the simplified-block format with open punctuation. Point out the differences between the simplified block format and the other two formats.)
  E. Business Envelopes (Use Figure 6-4 as a sample of a correctly addressed business envelope.)

II. Writing Letters with Neutral or Positive Messages
  A. Planning Letters with Neutral or Positive Messages
    1. Identify the objective.
    2. Identify the main idea.
    3. Determine the supporting information.
    4. Adjust the content to the receiver.
  B. Organizing Letters with Neutral or Positive Messages
    1. Main idea
    2. Supporting information
    3. Goodwill closing
  C. Writing Letters with Neutral or Positive Messages

1. Letters with neutral messages
   a. Routine requests (Use Figures 6-5 and 6-6 as examples of poorly written and well-written routine request letters. Ask students what is wrong with the letter in Figure 6-5—it uses the indirect order and only implies what it wants the receiver to do; it does not make it easy for the receiver to do what the sender wants.)
   b. Claims
2. Letters with positive messages
   a. Orders (Use Figure 6-7 as an example of a poorly written order letter. Ask students what is wrong with it. For example, its language is hazy and confusing; it is not clear what is being ordered; it does not say where to ship the merchandise; it does not state the total of the purchase. Use Figure 6-8 as an example of a well-written order letter. Use Transparency 6-8 as an example of a well-written positive response letter.)
   b. Positive responses to a request (Use the same process for Figures 6-9 and 6-10 as used for Orders and Routine Requests.)
   D. Goodwill Letters
      1. Friendship letters
      2. Acknowledgment letters
III. Writing Letters with a Negative Message
   A. Planning Letters with Negative Messages
      1. Identify the objective.
      2. Identify the main idea.
      3. Determine the supporting information.
      4. Adjust the content to the receiver.
   B. Organizing Letters with Negative Messages
      1. Neutral opening
      2. Reasons for the negative message
      3. The negative message
         a. Imply the negative message.
            (1) Use an "if" clause.
            (2) Use the passive voice.
            (3) Focus on what you can do rather than what you cannot do.
         b. Avoid personal pronouns when giving the negative message itself.
      4. Closing (Use Transparencies 6-6 and 6-7 as examples of poorly written and well-written bad-news letters. Ask students

what is wrong with the letter in 6-6—it uses the direct order, it is so short that it is offensive, and it has a very weak closing.)
   C. Writing Letters with Negative Messages
      1. Declining a request [Use Figure 6-11 as an example of a poorly written letter that declines a request. Ask students what is wrong with it—it is offensive in that it implies that the receiver cannot see well (signs posted all over the store), uses negative language when saying no, apologizes when the company did not make a mistake, and has a poor soft sale. Use Figure 6-12 as an example of a well-written letter that declines a request.]
      2. Refusing credit
   D. Writing Letters with Both Positive and Negative Messages
      1. Use the positive message as the opener.
      2. Give the reasons for the negative message after the positive message.
      3. After the reasons for the negative message, give the negative message.
      4. Provide a helpful, goodwill closing.

Classroom Strategies

Business letters are written documents that represent a company or organization and the person who wrote them. The ability to write good and accurate letters is an important business communication skill.

Students must learn to analyze each different situation and receive and adjust accordingly. The steps for planning a letter and the organizational patterns presented in this chapter work for most situations. Emphasize, though, that students must always consider their receivers and adjust for them if necessary.

Solutions to End-of-Section Activities

Discussion Questions

Section 6.1
1. The standard parts of a business letter are the dateline, letter address, salutation, body, complimentary close, writer's name and title, reference initials, and copy notation.

2. In the block format, all parts of the letter start at the left margin. In the modified block format, the dateline, the complimentary close, and the writer's name and title begin in the middle of the page. In the simplified block format, all parts of this letter begin at the left margin, but the salutation and the complimentary close are omitted.

3. The information in the letter address is identical to the information needed for the address on an envelope.

Section 6.2

1. The main idea should be placed in the first or second sentence of the letter. It is placed there so that the receiver will react positively to the message immediately.

2. a. Contains information about the items being ordered, such as catalog number of each item ordered; quantity of each item ordered; and descriptions including cost, size, and color; method of shipping, etc. Also should indicate where the order is to be shipped.

    b. Specifies information required to obtain a complete response, such as times, dates, benefits to the receiver, and terms of payment.

    c. Provides necessary information so that the receiver knows what the sender is offering and expects. It also makes necessary requests.

    d. May or may not be necessary. If necessary, the supporting information provides the necessary details the receiver needs in order to do what is needed.

3. It is important because it provides an excellent opportunity to increase goodwill with the receiver. In letters to customers, it provides an opportunity for a soft sale.

Section 6.3

1. The steps in planning a bad news letter are (1) identify the objective, (2) identify the main idea, (3) determine the supporting information, and (4) adjust content for the receiver.

2. It is used because it should prepare the receiver for the negative message, thus making the negative message more acceptable.

3. The purpose of the opening is to introduce the topic of the letter, the purpose of supporting information is to provide acceptable reasons for the negative message, and the purpose of the closing is to provide an opportunity to maintain or build goodwill or to provide a soft sale.

Solutions to End-of-Chapter Activities

Critical Thinking Questions

1. Formatting is important because it is the basis of the first impression of a letter. The better the formatting, the more positive the first impression of the receiver.

2. The opening of a letter with a neutral or positive message will make the message acceptable to the receiver. Thus, the receiver of this type message is psychologically ready and may even be happy to read the rest of the letter. The opening of a letter with a negative message introduces the topic of the letter. If the sender were to reveal the main idea of this type of message, the negative message, the receiver might not read the rest of the letter, which includes the reasons for the negative news.

3. Yes, the objectives are similar. They are generally written to maintain goodwill. The main ideas, though, will differ because they have different messages to deliver.

Applications

Part A.
1. claim
2. request
3. positive response
4. positive response
5. acknowledgment
6. claim

Part B. Letter Type–Positive Response. Direct Order. Main Idea–the products used are safe and efficient. Supporting Information–none needed but could provide examples of products used and their "safeness."

Part C. Letter Type–Positive Response. Direct Order. Main Idea–here is the information you requested. Supporting Information–the registration dates.

Part D. Letter Type–Acknowledgment. Direct Order. Main Idea–we have received your application. Supporting Information–thank you for your application; processing the application will take about ten days. Check format carefully.

Part E. Letter Type–Positive Response. Direct Order. Main Idea–your loan has been approved. Supporting Information–sign the loan agreement within 14 days. Check format carefully.

Part F. Letter Type–Acknowledgment. Direct Order. Main Idea–you have received her application. Supporting Information–thank you for the application; processing will take about two weeks. Check format carefully.

Part G. Letter Type–Positive Response. Direct Order. Main Idea–Ms. Bennett's application has been approved. Supporting Information–the account has a $500 limit; billing periods are 30 days; and the interest rate on the amount owed is 1.5 percent a month. Check format carefully.

Part H. Letter Type–Request Denial. Indirect Order. Main Idea–we cannot give you a refund. Supporting Information–the resume was printed as directed after proofreading. Check format carefully.

Part I. Letter Type–Acknowledgment. Direct Order. Main Idea–thank you for your order. Supporting Information–none needed. Check format carefully.

Part J. Letter Type–Positive and Negative Message. Indirect Order. Main Ideas (2)–we will send the drill sets today, and we will send the dish sets in two weeks. Supporting Information–we are temporarily out of the dish sets. Check format carefully.

Part K. Letter Type–Credit Denial. Indirect Order. Main Idea–we cannot give you a charge account. Supporting Information–you have many charge accounts, all at their limits. Check format carefully.

Part L. Letter Type–Request Denial. Indirect Order. Main Idea–we cannot refund your money. Supporting Information–the dress has been altered. Check format carefully.

Part M. Letter Type–Credit Denial. Indirect Order. Main Idea–the application for credit is denied. Supporting Information–you lack credit references. Check format carefully.

Editing Activities
Block format with open punctuation

April 14, 20—

Mr. Marvin Fontana
98 Barfield Road
Atlanta, GA 30328-5187

Dear Mr. Fontana

Welcome to First Bank. Enclosed is a brochure that will answer any questions you have about your new checking account.

Also enclosed is your "Everywhere" automated teller machine card. You can use your "Everywhere" card at any First Valley Bank branch. In addition, you can use it at any other teller machine that displays the "Everywhere" logo.

Thank you for choosing First Bank. We are pleased to be able to serve you by providing for your banking needs.

Sincerely

Nancy Tallman
Customer Service Representative

cp

Enclosures

Modified block with mixed punctuation

April 14, 20—

Mr. Marvin Fontana
98 Barfield Road
Atlanta, GA 30328-5187

Dear Mr. Fontana:

Welcome to First Bank. Enclosed is a brochure that will answer any questions you have about your new checking account.

Also enclosed is your "Everywhere" automated teller machine card. You can use your "Everywhere" card at any First Valley Bank branch. In addition, you can use it at any other teller machine that displays the "Everywhere" logo.

Thank you for choosing First Bank. We are pleased to be able to serve you by providing for your banking needs.

Sincerely,

Nancy Tallman
Customer Service Representative

cp

Enclosures

Case Studies

1. a. Should be a routine request letter written to the admissions office of a university asking for admissions materials, registration dates, and informational brochures.

   b. Should be a memo in simplified format with the following answers: The letter is a routine request. It should be written in the direct order. Its main idea is "Please send me. . . ." Its supporting information is the request for materials for admission, on registration dates, and on other information.

   c. Answers will vary but should be in simplified letter format and use the subject line "EVALUATION OF A UNIVERSITY."

   d. Students are to print a copy of your e-mail and give it to you.

2. A memo in the traditional format should contain the problems with the letter in Case 2. Problems are: (1) uses the indirect order, (2) reminds customer of her disappointment with product, (3) says nonverbally that the customer is careless, (4) says nonverbally that the customer is not deserving but sender will grant her desire anyway, (5) calls her a complainer (see title of sender). Show Transparency 6-8 as a possible solution to Case 2(b).

Career Case Studies

Communication for Engineering and Industrial Careers

1. Luisa is writing a letter that contains a negative message.

2. The letters should not be the same. Mr. Alfonso seems to be sensitive to the needs of others. Thus, his letter should be written using the indirect order. Mr. Johnson seems to be more concerned about time and the money associated with time. Thus, his letter should probably be changed and written in the more efficient order, the direct order.

Communication for Natural Resources and Agriculture Careers

1. You are sending a message that contains both a positive message and a negative message.

2. Open the message with a positive statement— the part of the budget that has been funded. Next, give the reasons the other parts of the budget were not funded, and name those parts. Close the message with helpful suggestions about what the rangers can do to cover the lack of funds. Or encourage the rangers to continue soliciting funds for park improvement.

Video Case

1. The following human qualities are revealed in the video and/or the case study: curiosity, ability to learn and embrace new technologies, empathy for customers, sense of humor, creativity, organizational knowhow, appreciation of others, gratitude, attention to detail, trustworthiness, and integrity.

2. Students can argue that it is only a coincidence that orders from long-term customers fell when Erika stopped sending letters to these customers. That argument is undercut by Erika's reaction— she is convinced of a connection. Students might infer that long-time customers liked the amount and form of communication. Students might write that, while long-term customers might use the new communication technologies Erika has adopted, they could also be missing the more traditional, personal form of letter correspondence.

3. Several times in the video the spokesman for Superior Livestock mentions customer service. He mentions trust. He is shown weeding out unhealthy cattle from a customer's order. Given this commitment, it is doubtful that Superior abandoned letter correspondence. Perceptive students might note that high-tech means of communication do not replace the more intimate advantages of hard-copy correspondence.

4. Student letters will vary. They may choose any format, but the letter should include essential elements (letter address, complimentary close, etc.). Students must also be clear about the objective and main idea of the letter. The tone of the letter should be friendly; and, given the purpose of the letter, it should contain a goodwill closing.

Continuing Case

1. Not quite. The letter is mostly in block format. However, the paragraphs should not be indented and they should be separated by a double space.

2. She presents basically a negative message, with a little positive news about the coffee aspect of the NetCafe.

3. Eva begins and ends the letter with a negative message. Instead, she needs to focus on what went well. For example, the computer aspect of the shop did show a small profit, but instead of

stressing that, she points out that it didn't meet its goal of $23,000. The good news about the coffee part of the business is buried late in the letter. She should stress the good news and present the bad news in as positive a way as possible.

4. Students' revised letters should begin with the positive message that both aspects of the shop made a profit. Next, they might point out the newness of the business. Then they should mention that, understandably, the computer aspect of the shop fell a little short of its goal of $23,000. (Students might make up a goal for the coffee counter, if they wish.) The letters should stress the approaches that Eva and Ramon are implementing to increase the shop's income.

Chapter 7
Researching and Using Information

Student Learning Objectives

Section 1
- List the basic steps in any research project.
- Define keywords and explain their use in an information search.
- Explain the purpose and importance of a timeline in planning a research project.

Section 2
- Identify primary and secondary sources of information.
- Discuss the resources available conducting research in public libraries.
- Explain how subject indexes and search engines are used in an information search on the Web.
- List the advantages and disadvantages of advanced search features.

Section 3
- Discuss a method of organizing and prioritizing research information in a report.
- Explain the importance of validity and reliability in evaluating research information.
- Identify the key copyright issues involved in using published information.

Teaching Outline

Introductory Points
- A successful search begins with solid planning.
- There are many sources of information and many ways to arrive at the same information.
- The Web is a wonderful source of information, but it is not necessarily always the best choice for a search.
- Information must be carefully evaluated before it is used.

I. Planning and Defining the Search
   A. Steps in a Search (Use Transparency 7-1.)
      1. Planning the search
      2. Locating sources of information
      3. Organizing the information
      4. Evaluating the sources
      5. Using the information
   B. Understanding the Assignment (Use Transparency 7-2.)
      1. What question must be answered?
      2. What information will be needed?
      3. What is the best method to use in locating this information?
      4. Where are the best sources of information?
      5. What is the first step?
      6. Ask clarifying questions if you cannot answer these questions.
   C. Using Keywords to Define the Focus of the Search
      1. Keywords are search terms that relate to the search topic.
      2. Creative-thinking techniques can help define the focus by developing related search terms. (Use Transparency 7-3.)
   D. Developing Deadlines and Timelines
      1. The timeline is a tool for planning and scheduling the phases of the project. (Use Transparency 7-4.)
      2. Develop the timeline by working backward from the project's deadline or due date.
II. Locating Sources of Information
   A. Secondary Information
      1. Secondary information is contained in published form.
      2. Secondary information can be found in books, periodicals, encyclopedias, dictionaries, handbooks, almanacs, directories, government publications, electronic databases, and web sites. (Use Transparency 7-5.)
      3. When analyzing information, it is important to distinguish between fact and opinion.
   B. Primary Information
      1. Primary information is unpublished and is gathered firsthand by the researcher.
      2. Primary information includes interviews, surveys, and observations.

C. Knowing Where to Look
1. Begin your search for information by reviewing secondary information.
2. Conduct primary information research if the project requires it.
3. As you gather information, keep notes, including bibliographical information, on index cards or pages.

D. The Library
1. There are many types of libraries, including public libraries, university libraries, business libraries, and public and private collections.
2. Libraries contain a multitude of resources, including librarians who are trained to assist with your research.

E. Finding It on the Web
1. Web sites are reached by keying the correct URL, or uniform resource locator, also known as the web address.
2. To locate web sites that may contain information relevant to your search, enter keywords in a search engine or subject index. (Use Transparency 7-6.)
3. Web searches result in a list of hits regarding your requested search. These lists may be very long.
4. Web rings can be valuable resources. They may include dozens or even hundreds of linked web sites, all on the same research topic.

F. Advanced Search Features
1. Boolean operators such as AND, OR, and NOT allow the researcher to either broaden or narrow the scope of the search.
2. Truncation and wild cards allow the researcher to search for a number of keywords that share the same root or base word.

III. Organizing, Evaluating, and Using Information
A. Organizing and Prioritizing Information
1. Organize the information you have gathered in a logical manner so that it flows from beginning to middle to end.
2. Form conclusions based on the facts you have gathered, and make recommendations based on those conclusions, if appropriate to the assignment.

B. Evaluating Sources of Information

1. Information should be evaluated constantly to make sure it is valid and reliable. (Use Transparency 7-7.)
2. Information should be current, not dated.
3. Information should be well balanced and unbiased.
4. Information sources should be reputable.

C. Using Information
1. Using the work of an author without authorization and without credit is a violation of copyright laws.
2. Plagiarism, or presenting the work of another as your own, is unprofessional and unethical.

Classroom Strategies

The ability to locate facts and data is vital to success in the workplace. Use this chapter to acquaint students with information search strategies. Encourage students to become familiar with library resources and to explore the Web to acquaint themselves with the various resources available and how they produce results.

The applications and case studies at the end of the chapter provide students with opportunities to review a variety of resource materials. Use these activities for discussion with students on how and why they selected the search strategies and keywords that they did, how successful each search was, and what they might change in future information searches. Compare search strategies selected by various students and point out that although they may have used different methods, they were able to arrive at the same information.

Solutions to End-of-Section Activities

Discussion Questions

Section 1

1. You should know the purpose of the research—what specific information you are seeking and the particular country that is the focus of your report. Ask yourself: What question am I trying to answer? What information will I need to answer this question? Where might I find the best sources on this topic? What is the most logical first step? How should I proceed?

2. Answers will vary on keywords. The list probably would have been more expansive if a creative-thinking technique had been used because it allows the mind to generate a large number of ideas in a short burst of creativity.

3. Answers will vary.

Section 2

1. Your method of research will depend primarily upon the focus of your search. If the information you need can be quickly and easily accessed on the Web, it might be more logical to conduct the research from your computer instead of visiting the library. If you require access to services that are available only at the library or are not easily accessed on the Web, or if you need help with your research, you might prefer to visit the library and consult the librarian for assistance.

2. Although you probably could find some books or articles about air traffic controllers, the best method of gathering information about the job would be to get firsthand information—either interviews or observations, or a combination of the two. By talking to air traffic controllers and possibly job shadowing an air traffic controller, you would get a much better picture of what the job involves.

3. Answers will vary but might include *job*, *work*, and *computer*. To limit the search to computer jobs in Atlanta, use the Boolean operator AND to limit the search. For example, you might enter *job* AND *computer* AND *Atlanta*.

Section 3

1. Possibly. Because *edu* indicates a site operated by an educational institution, such as a university, it generally would be considered a reputable site. A commercial site, which ends with *com*, is operated by a private individual or business and should be scrutinized closely to make sure the information is reliable.

2. Bias means the information is not well balanced. Bias can relate to age, gender, race, national origin, or simply a biased presentation of facts. To be reliable, information should be free of all bias.

3. To use the words of another person and present them as your own is called plagiarism; it is unprofessional and unethical. Using the original work of an author without crediting your source also is a copyright violation.

Solutions to End-of-Chapter Activities

Critical Thinking Questions

1. Nouns and verbs are used together to describe a fact. Adjectives and adverbs are often used to describe an opinion.

2. Without each phase of the research process being completed appropriately, the resulting report may present inadequate or incorrect data or may not provide the requested information. Planning needs to take place first to prepare properly for the search. Once information is located, it must be organized and evaluated before being used in a report. To eliminate any step along the way may result in a poorly produced project.

3. Interviews might be your first choice for a research method if you need to gather original firsthand information from interview subjects. Unlike a survey, the interview format allows you to ask clarifying questions, which can greatly expand the amount of information you receive.

4. Unlike publicly held companies, private companies are not required to disclose proprietary information. Therefore, you will not be able to access information that typically is included in a publicly held company's annual report. You will have to rely on other sources, such as business journals and newspapers, for information.

5. To more tightly focus your search, you could try using different keywords, or you could use the Boolean operator AND to narrow the search by requiring that all words connected by AND be present in each hit.

6. Dated information may no longer be relevant to your research. By including it, you could be misrepresenting facts and could confuse your readers. Before including dated information in your report, conduct an extensive search to make sure there are no resources available that offer more current data.

Applications

Part A. Answers will vary but may include some of the following:

1. employee benefits: sick leave, health insurance, retirement plan, life insurance, paid vacation, employee discount

2. customer service skills: smile, greeting, eye contact, offer to assist customer, tone of voice
3. office dress code: business attire, professional, casual, fabric, length of clothing, clothes with logos or slogans, dress-down day

Part B. Answers will vary depending on the selected topic.

Part C. Answers will vary depending on the selected topic. A sample e-mail might be:

Dear Ms. Newell:

I am preparing a report on customer service skills for a Business Communications class assignment. Because you are the regional training manager for the Kinko's Copy Centers in this area, I am certain you have a great deal of excellent information about customer service. I would appreciate the opportunity to spend 15 or 20 minutes with you to ask you a few questions for my report. Would you be available on September 12 at 3:30 p.m. for a brief interview in your office? If not, would another time be more convenient? My report is due on September 15. I would appreciate hearing from you as soon possible. Thank you.

Part D. Reports will vary depending on selected topic and information resources.

Part E. Answers will vary depending on the selected resources. Students should use the appropriate citation styles located in Appendix D.

Part F. Answers will vary but the reports should contain a ranking of banks based on their services.

Part G. Answers will vary. If rankings in Part F are changed, they must be justified.

Editing Activity

The e-mail does not indicate what "situation" the writer is referring to and does not provide the date he will be meeting with the president or the date by which he needs the report. Here is an example of a revised e-mail message:

Please prepare a report by 9:00 a.m. Monday morning, June 14, on the necessary roof repairs in our Midwest office. I will be meeting with the president on Monday afternoon and will need to review before that meeting the most current estimates on repair costs and completion time.

Case Studies

1. The information Greg needs regarding the percentage of foreign-born residents is available through the U.S. Census Bureau. Greg quickly accesses the appropriate web site by visiting the Internet Public Library reference center (www.ipl.org/div/subject/browse/ref00.00.00). From there, he follows the links to "Census Data & Demographics," "County and City Data Book" (tables describing aspects of the population of the 77 largest U.S. cities), and "Rankings of Large Cities."

   This site provides a table of cities with a population of 100,000 or more, ranked by 2000 population figures and by the population of two or more races. The table indicates that New York, New York, is ranked number 1 and Los Angeles, California, is ranked number 2. Houston, Texas, where Worldwide Interpreting is located, is number 4.

   After compiling the list of the top ten cities, Greg simply checks the Yellow Pages directory for each city for listings of other translating or interpreting services. Yellow Pages directories for each city can be accessed through his local public library or on the Web.

2. Dolores knows that the Food Safety Inspection Service, an agency of the U.S. Department of Agriculture (USDA), conducts the inspections at her company and regulates the sale of meat in the United States. She decides that the USDA is a good place to start to look for information on overseas sales.

   Dolores accesses the USDA's web site at www.usda.gov and checks for links. She clicks on a link to "Agencies, Services, and Programs" of the USDA and finds the Food Safety Inspection Service. A pull-down menu of available information at that site includes a link to "Library of Export Requirements."

   When Delores accesses the Library of Export Requirements, she is able to select "Country Requirements Alphabetical," which provides a full listing of requirements and restrictions presented alphabetically by country. She quickly accesses the pages for Russia, Korea, and Saudi Arabia, and prints the information for inclusion in her report.

Career Case Studies

Communication for Health Services Careers

1. Because the information Frank is seeking is not available from secondary sources, he must conduct primary research. Interviews haven't worked well in the past because of employees' reluctance to be candid about their reasons for leaving the employ of Mercy Medical. Therefore, a survey probably is the best method for gathering information in this case.

2. Frank needs to design his questionnaire carefully. Questions must be worded so that the participants will be willing and able to provide a thorough answer. He also needs to distribute and collect the surveys in a way that will provide those responding total anonymity and confidentiality.

Communication for Media and Visual Arts

1. Before she can select the newspapers, Denise must determine which areas of the country have the highest population of senior citizens. By accessing the U.S. Census Bureau web site (www.census.gov), she finds links that lead her to a statistical brief titled *The 65 Years and Over Population: 2000.* In that brief, Denise finds that nine states have one million or more residents age 65 or older. Those states are California, Florida, New York, Pennsylvania, Texas, Ohio, Illinois, Michigan, and New Jersey. However, the states with the highest percentage of total population age 65 or older are Florida, Pennsylvania, North Dakota, Rhode Island, West Virginia, Arkansas, Maine, Iowa, and South Dakota.

   By comparing the two state lists, Denise can readily see that Florida and Pennsylvania appear on both lists. She therefore concludes that Florida and Pennsylvania are the states where New Horizon should initially concentrate its advertising.

2. She then can access a list of newspapers by state by entering the Internet Public Library site (www.ipl.org) and selecting newspapers by state. After developing a list of the daily newspapers in the major cities within each state, she can proceed to locate information about each newspaper, such as circulation figures and advertising rates, that will help her rank the publications and prepare her final list to recommend to the client.

Although she could call each newspaper and request a media buyer's information package, a quicker way to locate this type of information is *Standard Rate and Data Service—Newspaper Advertising Source*, which Denise can find in the reference section of her local library.

Video Case

1. Black Diamond uses a variety of research methods:

   - Machinist refers to book during design—Secondary
   - Testers destroy parts in stress testing—Primary
   - Skier uses bindings on ski slope—Primary
   - Black Diamond staff reads industry magazines—Secondary
   - Salesperson asks clients what they need—Primary

   What is important here is that students understand the difference between secondary and primary research and the variety of research available.

2. Here is a sample list of primary and secondary research students might recommend to Isabel:

   - Read magazines focused on winter sports to spot trends—Secondary
   - Poll Hot Chill customers on their winter sports equipment buying habits—Primary
   - Network with store managers to learn their successes and mistakes—Primary
   - Visit competitors' web pages to learn the focus of their marketing—Secondary
   - Call manufacturers to gain tips on creating an equipment display area—Primary

3. As consumers, students can draw on their own experience buying sports equipment. Students are helping Isabel gather marketing data. They might ask climbers how much money they spend on equipment each year, which brands they prefer, or how often they replace their equipment. Students might ask the climbers where they buy their equipment (store name, local or distant) or how they decide what equipment to buy. Students could also ask what is most important to the climbers: the quality of the equipment, the price, or the service they receive.

4. A table comparing features and prices for harnesses and ropes might resemble the following:

Harnesses	Black Diamond	Misty Mountain	REI
Cost (Rate 1–3)			
Durability (Rate 1–3)			
Features (Rate 1–3)			
Reputation (Rate 1–3)			

Ropes	Blue Water	Mammut	Maxim
Cost (Rate 1–3)			
Durability (Rate 1–3)			
Features (Rate 1–3)			
Reputation (Rate 1–3)			

Continuing Case

1. Students should list the sites they located, along with the search engines and Boolean techniques they used to find them. Encourage them to draw diagrams to show the links they accessed.

2. The sites that students select should be legitimate coffee suppliers, as far as it's possible to tell. Students should be able to answer questions (a)–(f) for most or all the sites they choose. To answer question (f), they might list aspects such as a clear, engaging text; colorful, meaningful graphics; enough information to answer the questions of most potential customers; and an e-mail address so customers can obtain more information.

Chapter 8
Developing and Using Graphic and Visual Aids

Student Learning Objectives

Section 1
- Discuss why graphic aids are used in the communication process.
- Describe how to place and identify graphic aids in written documents.
- Explain how graphic aids can mislead an audience.

Section 2
- Choose the graphic or visual aid that will best accomplish your communication objective.
- Create tables to present cumbersome information in an organized, easy-to-follow format.
- Create the three types of charts often used in business reports.
- Create line and bar graphs in their various formats.
- Identify miscellaneous graphic and visual aids used in reports.

Section 3
- Choose an appropriate visual aid that will enhance your oral presentation and help the audience to better understand your message.
- Prepare visual aids to ensure they are well received by your audience.
- Use visual aids in a professional manner during your oral presentation.

Teaching Outline

Introductory Points
- Because most people remember what they see much longer and better than what they *hear*, graphic aids are important to know how to use as a means of improving communication skills.

- This chapter will help your students realize the importance of using graphic aids. They will learn how to use graphic aids in written documents and how to choose the best graphic aid based on the objective they hope to achieve.
- The chapter includes coverage of tables, charts (organization charts, flow charts, and pie charts), line graphs (single- and multiple-line graphs), bar graphs (simple bar, broken bar, multiple bar, and stacked bar), and miscellaneous graphic and visual aids (maps, photographs, and drawings).
- The final section of the chapter will teach your students how to (a) decide whether their oral presentation requires visual aids; (b) choose the best visual aids (posters, flip charts, transparencies, slides, computer presentations, objects, chalkboards, whiteboards, electronic whiteboards, and handouts); (c) prepare their visual aids; and (d) present their visual aids.

I. Purposes and Placement of Graphic Aids
   A. Why Use Graphic Aids?
   1. A graphic aid provides a visual representation of the words in your message.
   2. Graphic aids provide an efficient means of presenting dense amounts of information in a way that can help the audience understand your message.
   3. Because most people remember what they see much longer and better than what they hear, graphic aids are important for you to know how to use as you work to improve your communication skills.
   4. Communicators increasingly use the various types of graphic aids discussed in this chapter for three reasons:
      a. Audiences expect that messages should be delivered in clear, easy-to-understand, visually stimulating formats.
      b. Technology has made the creation and delivery of graphic aids easier and more accessible than ever before.
      c. Communicators recognize that the odds of keeping their audience's attention and getting their points across are much higher when they use graphic and visual aids.

B. Using Graphic Aids in Written Documents
   1. Placing graphic aids
      a. Decide whether the graphic aid should be placed within the body of your document or in an appendix.
      b. Place your statement referring to the graphic aid *before* the actual graphic aid appears.
      c. When the placement of the graphic aid is to be in the body of the document, place the graphic aid on the same page as its reference statement.
      d. When that is not possible, then place the graphic aid on the page immediately following its first mention.
      e. Avoid dividing a graphic aid between two pages.
   2. Identifying graphic aids: graphic aids can contain the following four parts:
      a. A unique number for referencing purposes
      b. A title for each graphic aid that describes its contents
      c. The graphic aid
      d. A source line
C. Using Graphic Aids to Mislead
   1. Because some readers will only skim your document, giving more attention to the graphic aids than to the written text, graphic aids often have more impact than their accompanying text.
   2. Your readers will usually remember visual images longer than written text.
   3. For these reasons, you must analyze your graphic aids to ensure you have designed them so that they present an accurate picture of what the data represents.
   4. Your ethical responsibility is to report data as clearly and accurately as possible. (Use Transparency 8-1.)

II. Developing Graphic Aids
   A. To choose the best graphic aid, you must identify the objective you hope to achieve and choose a graphic aid suited to that purpose. (Use Transparency 8-2.)
   B. A table is an arrangement of information into rows and columns for reference purposes.
   C. The three types of charts commonly used in business reports are

   1. Organization charts, which illustrate the relationships among employees in an organization. (Use Transparency 8-3.)
   2. Flowcharts, which are step-by-step diagrams of a procedure or process
   3. Pie charts, which show how the parts of a whole are distributed and how the parts relate to one another. (Use Transparency 8-4.)
D. The most common graph types are
   1. Line graphs, which are useful for showing changes in a quantity or value over time
      a. Single-line graphs show the movement of only one quantity or value over time.
      b. Multiple-line graphs show the movement of two or more quantities or values over time. (Use Transparency 8-5.)
   2. Bar graphs are used when you want your audience to be able to compare the data represented in the graph.
      a. A simple bar graph compares only one set of data. (Use Transparency 8-6.)
      b. The simple vertical bar graph indicates quantity by the height of the bar.
      c. A simple horizontal bar graph indicates quantity by the length of the bar.
      d. A broken bar graph is used to indicate omission of part of each bar if some quantities are so large that they would go off the chart.
      e. A multiple-bar graph is useful for comparing more than one set of data at various points in time. (Use Transparency 8-7.)
      f. A stacked bar graph divides each bar into the parts that contributed to each total bar. (Use Transparency 8-8.)
E. Miscellaneous Graphic and Visual Aids
   1. A map shows geographic relationships and is especially useful when your audience may not be familiar with the geographic areas in your report. (Use Transparency 8-9.)

2. A photograph is used to provide a realistic view of a specific item or place and to make the document more appealing to read.
3. A drawing is useful for communicating a complicated idea or a procedure.

III. Using Visual Aids for Oral Presentations
  A. Choosing the Best Visual Aids
    1. Posters and flip charts
    2. Transparencies, slides, and computer presentations
    3. Objects
    4. Chalkboards, whiteboards, and electronic whiteboards
    5. Handouts
  B. Preparing Your Visual Aids
    1. Keep your visual aids simple and brief.
    2. Make sure everything is large enough to read from anywhere in the room.
    3. Use color for emphasis.
    4. Always include a title; use a source line if necessary.
    5. Prepare an acceptable number of visual aids.
  C. Presenting Your Visual Aids
    1. Display your visual aids at the right time.
    2. Display the points on your visual aids at the right time.
    3. Practice using your visual aids before the audience arrives.
    4. Face the audience when using your visual aids.

Classroom Strategies

The ability to present ideas visually in written and oral presentations is vital to an individual's ability to communicate effectively in the workplace. Use this chapter to help students understand the importance of using visual aids to enhance and increase understanding of their spoken and written word. Familiarize students with the purpose and placement of graphic aids, on how to choose the best graphic type to communicate their message, and on how to use visual aids appropriately.

The applications and case studies at the end of the chapter provide students with opportunities to apply the material presented in the chapter. Use these activities to provide a forum for discussion with students on what they have learned about developing and using graphic and visual aids and to give them a chance to prepare visual aids on their own. Encourage class discussion of each visual aid prepared and used by your students in class in order to coach them on what they're doing correctly and what needs to be changed.

Solutions to End-of-Section Activities

Discussion Questions

Section 8.1

1. Because some readers will only skim your document, giving more attention to the graphic aids than to the written text, graphic aids often have more impact than their accompanying text.
2. Answers to this question will vary. Some may see it as a positive characteristic because visual images help keep the audience's attention and assist speakers in communicating their ideas. Others may see it as a negative characteristic because it encourages audiences' lazy tendencies to have to be entertained and to not have to work to understand.

Section 8.2

1. An organization chart is used to illustrate the relationships and official lines of authority and communication among employees and departments of an organization. A flowchart is a step-by-step diagram of a procedure or process. A pie chart shows how the parts of a whole are distributed and how the parts relate to one another.
2. Answers will vary.
3. Answers will vary. Examples from the various charting programs available in the Microsoft Office suite include Excel's charting feature, Word's charting and table options, and PowerPoint's mini-applications for organization charts and bar and line graphs. In addition, all of the Microsoft applications have drawing tools.
4. (a) No, the data do not differ; they are just presented in a different way. (b) You would use the stacked bar graph when comparing total sales of each quarter.
5. No, Peter Alexander is not a subordinate to Kathy Gillespie. Peter and Kathy are both subordinates to Shondra Davis.
6. Students' answers will vary.

Section 8.3

1. Answers will vary. Students should choose from posters, flip charts, transparencies, slides, computer presentations, objects, chalkboards, whiteboards, electronic whiteboards, and handouts.
2. The two extremes you should avoid are (1) preparing so many visual aids that your audience gets buried in them, and (2) preparing so few visual aids that your audience gets bored looking at the same ones for long periods of time.

Solutions to End-of-Chapter Activities

Critical Thinking Questions

1. Answers will vary.
2. Answers will vary.
3. Possible answers include (a) thinking the programs will be harder to learn than they actually are and (b) procrastination.
4. Answers will vary.
5. Answers will vary.

Applications

Part A. Students' answers will vary. You should receive an e-mail from each student with two charts attached. Some sample charts are shown below.

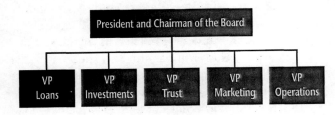

SOUTHCENTRAL BANK

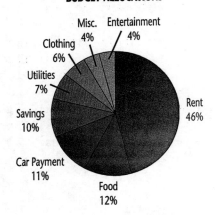

BUDGET ALLOCATIONS

Part B. Answers will vary.

Part C. Answers will vary.

Part D. Answers will vary.

Editing Activity

Possible solution:
1. Select what should be organized.
2. Get rid of clutter.
3. Break organizing tasks into specific steps.
4. Establish a simple system.
5. Stay organized.
6. Be only as organized as you need to be.

Case Studies

1. (a) Among the ideas Jan should consider are whether the current materials she is using are suitable for scanning for a PowerPoint presentation. How much work would it be for her to create from scratch those visual aids that are not suitable for scanning? Would it be appropriate to develop several versions of her presentation to use with various clients, based on what level of detail or which points need to be covered?

   (b) You should receive a printout of a picture from each student that demonstrates either handicap awareness or cultural diversity.

2. (a) Answers will vary.
   (b) Answers will vary.

Career Case Studies

Communication for Health Services Careers
Possible outline:
1. Introduction to Visual Aids
2. Importance to Communication Process
3. Choices Readily Available in Your Classroom
4. Demonstration of Use
5. Flip Charts
6. Overhead Projectors with Transparencies
7. Electronic Whiteboards
8. Points to Keep in Mind When Using Visual Aids

Communication for Business and Marketing Careers
1. Possible graphic aids include bar charts comparing the average cost for one-week vacation accommodations for hotels, camping out, and timeshare condominiums; and tables comparing

amenities that come with each of the vacation options. Possible visual aids include a miniature *flip chart* that would contain the various charts and tables mentioned above. If the salespeople present information to larger groups of potential buyers, they could use a *multimedia projector* to display the tables and charts prepared by using a program such as PowerPoint.

2. The multimedia projector would also allow video projection, should the resort wish to prepare a video of the resort and surrounding area to promote Branson as an excellent vacation destination. Handouts with necessary information could also be used. Photographs could be used to illustrate places at the resort that the sales force would not have time to show every potential buyer in person.

Video Case

1. Students might offer a range of topics. They might organize their outline functionally or chronologically. A sample outline follows:

   I. Preparation
      Research physical setting of presentation.
      Know your equipment.
      Know your audience.
   II. Opening
      Introduce yourself.
      Introduce topic.
   III. Body of Presentation
      Maintain relationship with audience through eye contact and nonverbal communication.
      Use graphic aids to show relationships, provide examples, and explain procedures.
   IV. Closing
      Restate crucial points.
      Reuse graphics to illustrate crucial points.
      Allow time for questions.

2. Students might offer a variety of tips. They might suggest the guidelines from the Prepare Your Visual Aid or Use Your Visual Aid sections of Chapter 8.

3. Answers will vary. Students should, however, mention that presentation audiences expect carefully chosen visual aids. A presentation composed of text only does not engage an audience.

4. I. Table
      Illustrates difference between homologous and autologous blood transfusion by defining both.
   II. Flowchart
      Shows steps in screening blood donors for infectious diseases.
   III. Bar Graph
      Shows comparison of common risks, comparing blood transfusions to automobile accidents, etc.
   IV. Pie Chart
      Showing comparison of blood type frequency.
   V. Photograph
      Showing Memorial Hospital's blood donation area, including its friendly staff.

Students need to be able to choose from the range of visual aids available.

Continuing Case

1. A pie chart offers the clearest way to show how the parts of a whole are distributed. Students should place the "coffee sales" wedge so its left edge lines up with the 12:00 position on the circle. The other wedges should be placed in descending order, clockwise.

2. To show trends over time, students might use a multiple-line graph. Students might also use a multiple-bar graph to compare income from various sources for each quarter. For either kind of graph, each quarter would be marked along the horizontal axis. The vertical axis would show income, starting at 0. For a line graph, each source of income would have its own line. For a bar graph, each source would have its own color of bar, with a cluster of bars for each quarter. Both kinds of graphs require a legend to identify what each line or bar represents.

3. Students should point out a gradual increase in income in all categories, with a bigger increase in the computer-related fees than in the coffee-counter income.

4. Possible answers: They might show how their income was spent, using a pie graph for the entire year and/or a line graph to trace spending trends from quarter to quarter. Eva and Ramon could develop a line graph that uses figures from the first year to predict the shop's income for the next six months. Perhaps they could use a map to show where most of their customers live or work.

Chapter 9
Writing Routine Reports

Student Learning Objectives

Section 1
- Explain how to classify reports according to their style, purpose, and format.
- Identify the steps in planning an informal report.
- Explain the difference between data, conclusion, and recommendation.

Section 2
- Explain when to use direct or indirect order to organize an informal report.
- Know when to use the personal and impersonal writing styles in informal reports.
- List the parts of an informal report.
- Describe when to use the letter, memo, and manuscript formats for informal reports.

Teaching Outline

Introductory Points
- A report is a document that provides facts about a specific situation or problem.
- Reports are business tools that enable managers to make decisions or solve problems; thus, they are critical to the effectiveness of an organization.
- Writing reports is a common practice in the workplace.

I. Planning Informal Reports
  A. Types of Reports
    1. Style
      a. Formal (In today's business world, formal reports are seldom written because they are time-consuming and expensive. However, they can be valuable to the receiver if their content is important and to the sender because they send a nonverbal message about the sender's abilities.)
      b. Informal (Point out that informal reports are much more common than formal reports.)
    2. Purpose
      a. Informational
      b. Analytical
    3. Format
      a. Memo (Use Transparency 9-2 to assist in the teaching of format for memo reports.)
      b. Letter (Use Transparency 9-1 to assist in teaching the format of a letter report and the parts of a report.)
      c. Manuscript
  B. Steps in Planning Informal Reports
    1. Identify the problem
    2. Decide on areas to investigate
    3. Determine the scope
    4. Plan the research
    5. Develop a preliminary outline
      a. Outlines for informational reports
        i. Chronological order
        ii. Order of importance
        iii. Logical sequence
        iv. Category
        v. Geographical order
      b. Outlines for analytical reports
        i. Hypotheses
        ii. Alternatives
      c. Outline systems (Use Figure 9-1 to provide an example of these outline systems.)
        i. Alphanumeric system
        ii. Decimal system
      d. Outline formats
        i. Topical outline
        ii. Discussion outline
    6. Collect the data
      a. Primary research
      b. Secondary research (To show examples of a bibliography and a note card, use Figure 9-2.)
        i. Bibliography cards
        ii. Note cards
    7. Analyze data, draw conclusions, and make recommendations
      a. Analyze data—data are facts and bits of information
      b. Draw conclusions—conclusions are opinions based on the interpretation of data

c.　Make recommendations—recommendations are suggestions on what should be done and should be based on conclusions

II.　Writing Informal Reports
　　A.　Organizing Informal Reports
　　　　1.　Direct order (Use Figure 9-3 as an example of an outline for an informational report using the direct order. Use Figure 9-4 as an example of an outline for an analytical report using the direct order.)
　　　　2.　Indirect order (Use Figure 9-5 as an example of an outline of an analytical report using the indirect order.)
　　B.　Outlining and Writing Informal Reports
　　　　1.　Report outlines
　　　　2.　Writing style
　　　　　　a.　Personal style
　　　　　　b.　Impersonal style
　　C.　Formatting Informal Reports
　　　　1.　Parts of an informal report
　　　　　　a.　Opening
　　　　　　b.　Body
　　　　　　c.　Closing
　　　　2.　Letter reports (Use Figure 9-6 to assist in the teaching of letter reports.)
　　　　3.　Memo reports (Use Figure 9-7 to assist in the teaching of memo reports.)
　　　　4.　Manuscript reports (Use Figure 9-8 to assist in the teaching of the content and formatting of a manuscript report.)

Classroom Strategies

Writing effective reports is an important tool for most business workers. Though the workers may not realize it, many memos and letters are reports. Because management views reports as one of its decision-making tools, reports must be informative and accurate.

The step-by-step approach presented in this chapter breaks down what can be a complex process into smaller steps that students can comprehend and apply. The questions at the end of the sections can be used to review these steps and their concepts. The applications at the end of the chapter encourage students to use the steps.

Solutions to End-of-Section Activities

Discussion Questions

Section 9.1
1.　Reports are classified according to style, purpose, and format so that we can use them as an effective communication tool.
2.　Yes, findings, conclusions, and recommendations differ. Findings are the basis on which we draw conclusions. Conclusions are the basis on which we make recommendations.

Section 9.2
1.　Reports are written in direct or indirect order because experience has taught us that, depending upon the kind of message you have to deliver, one of the orders will probably be more effective than the other.
2.　We know that in the business world we want to deliver reports as effectively and efficiently as possible. To meet these criteria, we have developed three formats for reports. Some are more efficient than others; but in certain situations, some are more effective than others. Thus, to write effective reports, we sometimes sacrifice a little efficiency.

Solutions to End-of-Chapter Activities

Critical Thinking Questions
1.　The steps for planning all types of informal reports are identical because they are necessary to prepare for the writing of a report. The preparation needed for writing a report, regardless of its type, is the same.
2.　The importance of business decisions based on informal reports is generally not as critical as the importance of business decisions based on formal reports. With so much at stake, these reports need to be impartial and professional. An impersonal style allows the reader to focus on the facts rather than on the writer.

3. All reports need to be planned carefully. To fail to do so could cause you to write an ineffective report. Yet, while planning is important to all reports, it is critical to long, complex reports. Without planning when writing this type of report, you may become confused and lost, and possibly fail to write an effective report.

Applications

Part A. Students' answers will vary. An example answer follows:

(1) Topic—the next purchase of wood to make furniture
(2) Problem Statement—Should Delbert Furniture Company purchase its next order of furniture wood from Sawmill A or Sawmill B?
Scope—The scope of this study will be limited to these two sawmills and to the price of the wood, ability of the sawmill to deliver the goods on time, and quality of the wood provided in past orders.
(3) Outline
  I. Introduction
    A. Introductory Sentences
    B. Problem Statement
    C. Scope
  II. Body (using Alternatives)
    A. Price of Wood
      1. Sawmill A
      2. Sawmill B
      3. Conclusion on Price
    B. Ability to Deliver
      1. Sawmill A
      2. Sawmill B
      3. Conclusion on Ability to Deliver
    C. Quality of Wood
      1. Sawmill A
      2. Sawmill B
      3. Conclusion on Quality of Wood
  III. Closing
    A. Summary
    B. Recommendation
(4) Alternatives were used because they allow for a better structure to present the data, draw conclusions, and make a recommendation.

Part B. Students' answers will vary. An example answer follows:

The data were contained in memos and invoices of Delbert Furniture Company. Invoices of May 13, July 19, September 3, October 29, and December 20 indicated that Sawmill A's prices per linear foot were $10.75, $11.02, $9.90, $10.15, and $12.12. During those same times, Sawmill B's prices per linear foot were $10.74, $11.45, $10.29, $10.39, and $12.49. A memo from the Delbert's furniture-construction supervisor indicated that both sawmills provided wood of excellent quality. However, the same memo indicated that in the past Sawmill A responded to an order and delivered wood more quickly than Sawmill B.

Part C. Students' answers will vary, but the report should contain conclusions and recommendations and should be in memo format. An example answer follows:

The data in Part B led to the following conclusions: Sawmill A generally has the best price, the quality of the wood from both sawmills is excellent, and Sawmill A has a better delivery record. Thus, the recommendation is to buy the wood from Sawmill A.

Part D. Possible solution is provided on Transparency 9-3.

Part E.
1. Students' answers will vary. An example answer follows:

PARKING FACILITIES AT OUR SCHOOL

  I. Parking Permits Required
    A. Yearly Permits Issued
    B. Yearly Fee of $10
    C. Display Permit on Rear Bumper
  II. Opinion Survey
    A. Students Are Not Satisfied with Parking Facilities
    B. Faculty Are Somewhat Satisfied with Parking Facilities
  III. Temporary Visitor Parking
    A. Register Visiting Vehicles
    B. Daytime Parking Only
    C. Visitor Parking Lots
      1. Lot 8 for Student Visitors
      2. Lot 5 for Faculty Visitors
  IV. Parking Enforcement
    A. Lots Patrolled Hourly
    B. Cars Checked when Entering Lots
    C. Cars without Permits Ticketed
    D. Cars with Three Unpaid Tickets Towed

2. The order selected for the report would depend upon how the writer thinks the receiver will respond to the report. If the receiver will have to be persuaded or will react negatively to the report, the indirect order should be used. If the receiver will react favorably or neutrally, the report should be in direct order. In this situation, because it is an informative report, the direct order should be used.

3. PARKING FACILITIES AT OUR SCHOOL
   I. Parking Permits Required
      A. Yearly Permits Issued
      B. Yearly Fee of $10
      C. Display Permit on Rear Bumper
   II. Temporary Visitor Parking
      A. Register Visiting Vehicles
      B. Daytime Parking Only
      C. Visitor Parking Lots
         1. Lot 8 for Student Visitors
         2. Lot 5 for Faculty Visitors
   III. Parking Enforcement
      A. Lots Patrolled Hourly
      B. Cars Checked when Entering Lots
      C. Cars without Permits Ticketed
      D. Cars with Three Unpaid Tickets Towed
   IV. Opinion Survey
      A. Students Are Not Satisfied with Parking Facilities
      B. Faculty Are Somewhat Satisfied with Parking Facilities

   The Opinion Survey is moved to the end of the report because (1) it might bias readers as they read the report, and (2) it is probably viewed by readers as the most important part of the report.

4. Because this is an informative report, the main idea is the information about the parking facilities and how students and faculty feel about them.

5. The problem statement of this report would be "The purpose of this report is twofold: (1) to inform students and faculty about our parking facilities, and (2) to reveal how they feel about them."

6. Answers will vary.

Editing Activities

1. The secondary sources should appear in bibliographic format and in alphabetic order according to authors' names.

   Carnegie, Dale. *How to Win Friends and Influence People.* New York: Simon & Schuster, 1998.

   Goldsmith, Joan and Kenneth Cloke. *Resolving Conflicts at Work.* San Francisco: Jossey-Bass, 2000.

   Gray, John. *How to Get What You Want and Want What You Have.* New York: Harper Trade, 2000.

   [Corrected words and phrases are underlined.]

2. Here is the report you requested on recommended electronic message systems for your organization. After surveying the number and types of messages your company sends, I recommend that you consider adding e-mail and fax machines. Because your organization sends many memos among eight branch offices, e-mail would speed up communication. Additionally, it would be inexpensive and convenient.

   Your offices often send illustrations and graphics to each other. Facsimile machines would speed up the process, provide high-quality imaging, and keep costs low.

Case Studies

1(a). The correct student response is to write an informal, informative report using the indirect order. Of course, because the report is informal, the student should indicate that he or she would use the personal style in the memo format. The reasoning behind these choices is that the sender is writing to someone within the company whom he or she knows well (an assumption because the writer is the manager of the shop). The indirect approach should be used because the writer can use the good news items in the initial part of the report, followed by the bad news items, closing with a summary. This approach buries the bad news and, hopefully, will soften it to some extent. Also, by using the personal style, focus is somewhat taken off the facts and placed on the people.

1(b). Answers will vary but should follow the guidelines given in 1(a).

2. The answers to this case will vary based upon the edition and articles selected. Student responses should be in memo format and contain at least four parts.

Career Case Studies

Communication for Health Services Careers

1. In this situation, your dilemma is that the major portion of your spouse's income comes from dental work for children. If you write the report and recommend the implementation of a fluoride system, you could cut your spouse's income by at least 50 percent.

2. Yes. Not to write the report would be selfish and unethical.

Communication for Engineering and Industrial Careers

1. Yes, it would be a good idea. However, it would also be a good idea to write a paragraph of explanation that should follow the figures in the report.

2. If the figures were negative, using a form containing the figures and then following them with an explanatory paragraph would mean that you would be using the direct order for a negative-news situation. This situation would not follow an accepted norm for business communication.

Continuing Case

1. One example: This report will analyze ways that older people can benefit from the services offered by the NetCafe and suggest ways to make them aware of these benefits. Another example: This report will answer the question, "Why do older people hesitate to visit the NetCafe and what can we do about it?"

2. The students' possible areas to investigate should closely relate to the problem statement they wrote for Question 1. For the purposes of this report, students might select just one or two areas to explore.

3. Students should set the boundaries of their reports, naming specific topics they will and will not cover.

4. Students should list the sources they will tap for information.

5. The outlines should follow a recognizable order, such as order of importance or categories of information.

6. If you have students complete this step, provide time for them to access various research sources.

7. Students' conclusions and recommendations should flow logically from the data they gathered. They should make specific suggestions concerning the services or approaches to be used or avoided at the NetCafe.

Chapter 10
Writing Formal Reports

Student Learning Objectives

Section 1
- Decide when to use a formal report.
- Prepare the possible preliminary and supplementary parts of a formal report.

Section 2
- Name the two types of special reports.
- Identify basic reports to management.
- Designate the three principal technical reports.

Teaching Outline

Introductory Points
- Formal reports can be major tools for promotion.
- Writing special reports is a common occurrence for many employees.
- Written reports are tools that management uses to help identify employees that are strong candidates for promotion.

I. Writing Formal Reports
  A. Planning, Organizing, and Writing Formal Reports
    1. Formal reports generally are more complex and longer than informal reports.
    2. Use a style manual to format a formal report.
       a. Company style manual
       b. MLA
       c. APA
       d. *Chicago Manual of Style*
    3. Direct and indirect order
    4. Writing style
  B. Parts of a Formal Report (To assist the teaching of the parts of a formal report, use Figure 10-1.)
    1. Preliminary parts
       a. Letter or memo of transmittal (Use Figure 10-2 for an example of a memo of transmittal.)
       b. Title page (Use Transparencies 10-1 and 10-2 here to help students with title pages. Emphasize the content of a title page and the benefits of a picture on a title page. Also emphasize that this is the first thing the receiver will see when receiving a formal report.)
          i. Without a picture
          ii. With a picture
       c. Table of contents (Use Transparency 10-3 to assist your teaching of the content and format of a table of contents.)
       d. Executive summary (sometimes called an abstract or synopsis) (Use Transparency 10-4 to provide an example of an executive summary.)
    2. Report Body
       a. Introduction (Use Transparency 10-5 here to assist you in teaching the content of an introduction and its format.)
          i. Authorization
          ii. Statement of the problem (objective)
          iii. Scope
          iv. Limitations
          v. Definitions
       b. Body
          i. Findings and analysis (Transparency 10-6 can be used here to help you teach the content of and appearance of the findings and analysis section of a formal report.)
          ii. Summary, conclusions, and recommendations
       c. Ending (Use Transparency 10-7 here to help your teaching of a summary, conclusions, and recommendations section of a formal report.)
    3. Supplementary Parts
       a. Bibliography (Use Transparency 10-8, which provides an example of a bibliography of a formal report. It is in MLA style.) (Appendix D

contains examples of APA and *The Chicago Manual of Style* entries for bibliographies.)
- b. Appendix (Use Figure 10-10 as an example of an appendix of a formal report.)
- C. Formatting Formal Reports
  1. Margins
  2. Spacing
  3. Headings (Use Figure 10-11 to assist your teaching of the use of headings.)
  4. Visual aids (See Chapter 8.)
II. Writing Specialized Reports
- A. Types of Specialized Reports
  1. Managerial reports
  2. Technical reports
- B Managerial Reports
  1. Staff reports
     - a. Introductory material
     - b. Summary
     - c. Objective
     - d. Findings
     - e. Analysis
     - g. Conclusions
     - h. Recommendation
  2. Status report (Sometimes called a progress report. This type of report is commonly used to report on the status of a project.)
  3. Audit report (Use Figure 10-13 as an example of an audit report.)
  4. Periodic report (Use Transparency 10-9 to provide an example of a periodic report.)
  5. Plan of action
- C. Technical Reports
  1. Analyses of alternatives (This type of report is an analytical report that analyzes alternatives and usually recommends an alternative to be implemented to solve a problem.)
  2. Systems white paper (This type of report is an informative report that provides information about a technology. The language used in the paper depends upon the ability of the receiver. For example, if the receiver has a technological background, the writer could use technical language. If the receiver does not, the writer could not use technical language.)

3. Annual report (A report required for all publicly held companies.)
   - a. A summary of the company's financial data over the past five to ten years
   - b. A discussion and analysis of the results of the company's operations and its financial condition
   - c. Recent stock prices
   - d. Summaries of unaudited, quarterly, financial data

Classroom Strategies

The ability to write reports is an important ability for most workers. Although a worker will not have to write formal reports often, when required, it will be very important. Receivers of formal reports generally are important clients of or officers within an organization.

Specialized reports are common writing tasks within an organization, but their importance should not be underestimated. They illustrate an employee's willingness and ability to do the common, but needed, activity. They also provide a written record of an employee's ability to write and communicate.

Effective use of the transparencies for this chapter can help students understand the content that goes into one of these reports and the format used. Use the activities and cases at the end of the chapter to develop analytical and report-writing skills.

Solutions to End-of-Section Activities

Discussion Questions

Section 10.1

1. It is important to have the purpose of the report in its introduction so that the receiver knows at the beginning of the report what it is trying to accomplish.
2. Headings are an important part of a long, formal report because they
   - a. break a big bundle of thought into smaller more digestible parts
   - b. illustrate what the report writer did to achieve the report's objective; i.e., the logic used to solve a problem

Section 10.2

1. Managerial reports and technical reports are similar in their general purpose: they are to inform management so that effective decisions can be made. They differ in that managerial reports are generally short and somewhat simple. Most technical reports are longer than managerial reports and usually contain technical, detailed information.

2. Managerial reports are very important to the writer. They provide a written record that management uses to determine the writer's ability to communicate.

3. Because the main ideas of analyses of alternatives and annual reports can be good news, bad news, persuasive, or routine, these kinds of reports can use any order. The main idea of a systems white paper is to present information on a technology. Thus, this type of report is considered routine and informational and uses direct order.

Solutions to End-of-Chapter Activities

Critical Thinking Questions

1. It is important to know how and when to write a long, formal report because when you do write them, they are very important. The receivers of long, formal reports usually are your supervisors, upper management, or CEOs, etc. As a result, your report is important to your career.

   Knowing when and when not to write a formal report is important also because they take a great deal of time to prepare. If you do not need to write one but do so, you will waste a great deal of time. Your supervisors would not be happy with your decision because of the wasted time. Also, they might suspect that you are trying to impress rather than express your thoughts.

2. A letter or memo of transmittal is important because it says basically, "Here is your report." Also, because it will be the first item in the report that your receiver will read, it provides the first impression about the report by your receivers. Yes, it could be written using personal pronouns because it needs to sound friendly and personable.

3. Student responses will vary. A possible answer would be

   They are all equally important because each report has a purpose to its recipients. For example, to the stockholder, the auditor, and company management, the audit report is extremely important because it reflects the financial condition of the company that was audited.

4. Status and periodic reports can differ in their usage. The purpose of a status report is to reveal the progress on a project; this type of report should be prepared using a sporadic time period. A periodic report is a report that can reveal the progress on a project; however, it may have other purposes (e.g., monthly sales report). Thus, a status report and a periodic report may have a similar or differing purpose. But one difference for sure is that a periodic report has a definite period of time that it covers (e.g., a *monthly* sales report has a definite time frame).

Applications

Part A

1. Unlike informal reports, formal reports use an impersonal writing style. A formal report will also be longer and will follow different formatting guidelines.

2. Yes, the report should have a section on findings and analysis because that was part of the assignment. However, because students were asked to write an informational report and not an analytical report, they are not authorized to make recommendations.

3. Secondary research sources will appear in the bibliography, which is one of the supplementary parts of the formal report.

4. The following is a possible outline of the formal report:

Parking Facilities at Our School
I.   Preliminary Parts
   A.   Letter or Memo of Transmittal
   B.   Title Page (with or without picture)
   C.   Table of Contents
   D.   Executive Summary

II. Report Body
  A. Introduction
  B. Body
    1. Parking Permits Required
      a. Yearly Permits Issued
      b. Yearly Fee of $10
      c. Display Permit on Rear Bumper
    2. Opinion Survey
      a. Students Are Not Satisfied with Parking Facilities
      b. Faculty Are Somewhat Satisfied with Parking Facilities
    3. Temporary Visitor Parking
      a. Register Visiting Vehicles
      b. Daytime Parking Only
      c. Visitor Parking Lots
        i. Lot 8 for Student Visitors
        ii. Lot 5 for Faculty Visitors
    4. Parking Enforcement
      a. Lots Patrolled Hourly
      b. Cars Checked when Entering Lots
      c. Cars without Permits Ticketed
      d. Cars with Three Unpaid Tickets Towed
  C. Summary, Conclusions, and Recommendations
III. Supplementary Parts*
  A. Appendix

*A bibliography probably would not be part of this report.

Part B. Student answers will vary. However, this report would probably be a memo report using the direct order and contain the information given in the activity. Be sure a correct memo format is used.

Part C
1. Surveys will vary. However, one should focus on the possible reactions of local residents and the other should focus on the possible reactions of students.
2. No answer necessary for this part of the assignment.
3. The status report to the president of the student body could probably be in any format—depending upon how students view their relationship with this individual. The status report to the leader of the local community should be in letter or manuscript format.
4. Student answers will vary but should be in formal report format with impersonal language. Be sure to check format.

Part D. Student answers will vary. However, the report should contain a plan of action that recommends purchasing the linens and selecting a laundry to clean them every week. The restaurant would save just under $27,000 a year by buying and sending them to a laundry twice a week. Be sure a correct format is used and that the report contains two graphics.

Editing Activities
[Corrected words or phrases are underlined.]
1. Before starting a project, check the list of existing templates and <u>see</u> if one of them <u>is</u> close to what you want. You can save <u>a lot</u> of time by making a few changes to an existing <u>template</u> instead of starting <u>from scratch</u>. As you <u>create</u> projects of your own<u>,</u> those saved documents will also become templates <u>that</u> can be easily changed and used for future occasions.
2. A memory function is <u>particularly</u> useful <u>when</u> using pictures that are selected from a floppy disk or CD. When using this <u>function</u>, it embeds a copy of the picture files used in your project within the project file <u>itself</u>; so, the <u>original</u> picture file is not required the next time <u>you</u> open the file. Thus, when selected<u>,</u> the package will not require you to insert the floppy disk or CD containing the picture used each time you open your project.

Case Studies
1. Student reports will vary. Nevertheless, this report should be a status report giving the details of the submitted lease proposals. Also, the report should indicate that Sandies Shops has not submitted its proposal.
2. Student reports will vary. However, they should provide the status of each dress and indicate that this group is in good shape for the show. It should also indicate that the writer intends to call companies that are providing the accessories for dresses 5, 9, and 10.

Career Case Studies

Communication for Natural Resources and Agriculture Careers
Student reports will vary. This report should identify alternatives and analyze each one and recommend one.

Communication for Business and Marketing Careers

1. Student reports will vary. Preliminary and supplementary parts for this proposed report should be identified and their reasons for inclusion in the report justified.

2. Student answers will vary but should contain an outline of a plan of action.

Video Case

1. Answers will vary. Students might pick and choose from Shaun's more formal, impersonal suggestions or Heather's less formal, more personal style—for example, a letter report with an impersonal tone. As long as students understand the reason for choosing one report form over another, several combinations can be argued.

2. Tone is important because Heather and Shaun are asking Krell Industries to donate resources to the Pedals for Progress 20K Ride. Heather and Shaun must argue their point without sounding presumptuous. They are essentially writing a proposal.

3. Depending on what report characteristics the student selects, the outline could include the executive summary of a formal report or the brevity of a letter report. Students might choose a topical outline or a discussion outline. Given that Heather and Shaun are asking Krell to donate money and time, any outline should include reasons for the donation and advantages to the company.

Continuing Case

1.
   a. Probably. A letter of transmittal to the two partners would add a personal touch.
   b. Yes, as this is required for a formal report.
   c. Yes, this is required for a fairly long report so readers can find certain sections.
   d. Yes, this is for Opal's benefit, as she doesn't want a lot of detail.
   e. Yes, this is an important part of an annual report.
   f. Yes, this is part of an annual report.
   g. Yes, this is part of an annual report.
   h. Yes, this is part of an annual report.
   i. Yes, this is part of an annual report.
   j. Probably not, as this is not a research report.
   k. If students say yes, they must suggest specific material to be included.

2. No, personal pronouns are not used in a formal report.

3. Yes, it should include shortcomings in order to present a balanced picture of the business.

4. It could include all three. The summary would briefly restate the main points of the previous information; the conclusions would explain what is working and what isn't; the recommendations might suggest making changes, such as adding more services or staff or dropping some.

5. Opal is impatient with details, so she will probably read the executive summary and perhaps the summary, conclusions, and recommendations.

6. Dominic is still dubious about the new business and may be worried about his money; so he is likely to study the whole report, especially the financial sections.

Chapter 11 Technical Communication

Student Learning Objectives

Section 1
- List the components of effective instructions.
- Describe how to write effective steps for instructions.
- Explain how a manual is similar to and different from instructions.
- Describe how to make information in a manual easy to locate.

Section 2
- Explain how a process description differs from a set of instructions.
- Describe the components of object and mechanism descriptions.
- Explain how to write a description of an object or a mechanism.
- List the components of a process description.

Section 3
- Plan a persuasive letter.
- Organize a persuasive letter.
- Organize a sales letter and a collection letter.
- Plan and organize a proposal.
- Organize a newsletter.

Teaching Outline

Introductory Points
- Letters, memos, and reports can be organized in different ways to serve a wide range of purposes, including writing to instruct, to describe, and to persuade.
- Technical writing usually requires precise language and careful organization. However, the key to all good business writing is putting the readers' needs first.

I. Writing to Instruct
  A. The Purpose of Instructions and Manuals
  B. Components of Effective Instructions (Use Transparency 11-1. Have students critique these instructions.)
    1. Clear and limiting title
    2. Introduction and list of needed tools or materials
    3. Numbered steps in sequential order
    4. Conclusion
  C. Guidelines for Writing Effective Steps
    1. Number the steps and start each one with a verb.
    2. Put the steps in sequential order.
    3. Describe each step separately.
    4. Indent any explanations.
    5. Describe special conditions first.
    6. Group steps under subheadings.
    7. Single-space within steps; double-space between them.
    8. Include graphics.
    9. Highlight warnings.
    10. Create a clear, inviting format.
    11. Have someone try out your instructions.
  D. Writing Effective Manuals: Making Information Accessible (Use Transparencies 11-2 and 11-3. Have students critique these instructions.)
    1. Detailed table of contents
    2. Introduction
    3. Tabs or dividers
    4. Graphics and diagrams
    5. Modifications for different experience levels
II. Writing to Describe
  A. Types of Description Writing
    1. Description
    2. Object
    3. Mechanism
    4. Process
  B. Components of an Object or Mechanism Description
    1. Clear and limiting title
    2. Introduction and overview
    3. Part-by-part description
    4. Conclusion
  C. Guidelines for Writing Object and Mechanism Descriptions (Use Transparencies 11-4 and 11-5.)
    1. Describe the object by its shape, dimensions, color, position, and so on.
    2. Be objective.

3. Be specific and precise.
4. Compare the unfamiliar to the familiar.
   D. Writing a Process Description: the Components
      1. Clear and limiting title
      2. Introduction
      3. Step-by-step description
      4. Conclusion
III. Writing to Persuade
   A. Purpose of Persuasive Writing
   B. Planning a Persuasive Letter
      1. Identify the objective.
      2. Identify the main idea.
      3. Determine the supporting information.
      4. Adjust the content to the reader.
   C. Organizing a Persuasive Letter (Use Transparency 11-6. Critique content of transparency.)
      1. Gain the reader's attention.
      2. Show the reader that he or she has a need.
      3. Explain your solution to that need.
      4. Present the supporting information.
      5. End by asking for specific action.
   D. Writing Different Kinds of Persuasive Messages
      1. Sales letters (Use Transparency 11-7. Critique content of transparency.)
      2. Collection letters
         a. Reminder stage
         b. Strong reminder stage
         c. Discussion stage
         d. Urgency stage
   E. Writing Proposals
      1. Planning a proposal
      2. Organizing a proposal
      3. Formatting a proposal
   F. Organizing a Newsletter
      1. Headlines
      2. Article titles
      3. Columns of text
      4. Pictures

Classroom Strategies

Students need to be able to apply a variety of organizational strategies to the writing tasks that will be required of them. In this chapter, they learn how to organize and write instructions and manuals; descriptions of objects, mechanisms, processes; persuasive letters and memos; proposals; and newsletters. Explore with students the possible situations in which employees in various positions and businesses might need to use these different forms of communication.

The critical thinking questions, applications, and case studies at the end of the chapter provide students with opportunities to apply the concepts and organizational techniques from this chapter to realistic situations. As students complete each item, discuss why they answered as they did. Remember that, in some situations, a range of responses may be appropriate.

Solutions to End-of-Section Activities

Discussion Questions

Section 11.1

1. The components are a clear and limiting title, an introduction and list of needed tools or materials, numbered steps in sequential order, and a conclusion.
2. Writers sometimes wrongly assume that readers will know who is to follow the instructions and under what conditions. Writers are also sometimes impatient to get started writing the instructions.
3. The most difficult part is seeing the task from the readers' point of view, including what they need to know in the instructions without offering too much detail and without omitting essential steps or information.
4. Your instructions were not as clear as you intended and could be interpreted in ways you did not anticipate. Or you might have wrongly assumed some kind of knowledge on the part of the reader.

Section 11.2

1. The components of all three types of descriptions are a clear and limiting title, an introduction and overview, a part-by-part or step-by-step description, and a conclusion.
2. Both figures focus on the same objects: floppy disks. Figure 11-2, the object description, explains what the parts look like and how they fit together, briefly summarizing their function. Figure 11-3, the process description, names the parts without describing them physically; instead, this description explains how the parts work together to accomplish a task.

3. Possible examples include advertisements, product brochures, instruction manuals, equipment specifications, and government regulations.
4. The terms *parallel to* and *rectangular* are clear and specific. The terms *nearby* and *several* are too vague to provide a clear picture of an object or mechanism.

Section 11.3
1. You must figure out what motivates others—what needs they have—in order to persuade them. A reason or benefit that motivates you will not necessarily motivate your readers.
2. If you ask for something in the beginning of a letter or memo, the reader might turn you down based on his or her understanding of the situation. Instead, you must stress the need for something first, so the reader can better understand why this request is important and be prepared to grant or approve it.
3. An unsolicited proposal is usually more difficult to write because you must establish a need for whatever you are proposing. However, some solicited proposals are also tricky to write; the RFP might be hard to follow or ask for information you do not have or would rather not share.

Solutions to End-of-Chapter Activities

Critical Thinking Questions
1. No, she is wrong. She is making her readers work to figure out the instructions rather than writing them in a numbered, step-by-step format, which would be easier to follow.
2. The length of any set of instructions or manual depends on the readers' needs. Longer might be better for someone who is unfamiliar with the task, while more experienced readers might want a shorter set of instructions.
3. Answers will vary, depending on the students' field of work. Nevertheless, they probably will need to write both instructions and process descriptions at some point in their careers.
4. Answers will vary. Descriptions in product brochures tend to fall in a category of their own.
5. Possible responses: The message should be organized in a direct way if the writer knows the reader prefers this approach or if the reader is likely to grant the request.

Applications

Part A. The maps that students drew in response to their partners' written directions should match the maps drawn by their partners. If not, the written directions may be unclear, perhaps interpretable in several ways. Have the partners work together on any necessary rewriting until they both agree that the directions are now clear. They could test their skill by asking a third student to read the directions and draw a map.

Part B. Students' answers will vary. The descriptions and presentations of the instructions should describe the process in general terms of how it happens and what it accomplishes, rather than how to carry it out.

Part C. Each student might give his or her rewrite of the partner's process to a third student. The third student will read the rewrite and try to explain the process orally. Have students determine whether there is enough clearly presented information in the rewrite for the third student to understand what is happening.

Part D. Ideally, students will be able to use the information in their partners' descriptions to identify the object or mechanism.

Part E. Invite students to share their rewrites with the class. Ask them to begin by pointing out the weaknesses in the original version.

Part F. The team's proposals should clearly outline a need felt by the high school administrators that will be met by adding a course or changing the schedule. Possible needs include using the faculty or the facilities more efficiently, adding a focus area to the school's offerings, and so on. Proposals also should clearly describe the proposed change, its costs, and timelines.

Part G. Students' letters should follow the pattern described in the text. The first reminder will be friendly. The second stage reminder might remind the customer of the need to preserve his credit rating. The discussion stage message seeks payment or an explanation. The urgency stage message advises the customer of the consequences of not paying.

Part H. This sales letter should gain the reader's attention, establishing a need, showing how a product or service will meet that need, presenting supporting information, and providing for an easy way for the reader to respond.

Part I. Students' newsletters should begin by describing several needs of the employees that will be met by joining the new sports team. Possible needs include getting more exercise, socializing with coworkers in a relaxed setting, and learning or strengthening a sports skill.

Editing Activities

1.
    1. Turn on the printer.
    2. Choose File Find File.
       The Search dialog box will open.
    3. Make sure that the File Name box contains *.doc.
    4. Click the down arrow by the Location box.
    5. Select the disk drive where your files are located.
    6. Click the OK button.
       The computer will search for the files.

2. What if you became v<u>e</u>ry sick at work? Your health—ev<u>e</u>n you<u>r</u> life—might depend on immediate help being nearby. For this reason, the company is offe<u>r</u>ing training in CPR, or cardiopulmonary resuscitation, to all employees who work he<u>re</u>. The co<u>u</u>rse will be held on two Tue<u>s</u>day evening<u>s</u> from 6:30 to 9:30 <u>p</u>m. The<u>re</u> is no charge. Many people have expre<u>s</u>sed <u>an</u> interest in the class, so sign up in the Human Resources office before the course get<u>s</u> filled. If you take the time to learn CPR, you may save someone's life at work or at home!

Case Studies

1. Students' answers will vary. An example answer follows: The employees will probably be overwhelmed by the amount of detail and the technical terms that Cassandra included in the instructions. They may be unable to follow them. Moesha might have been trying to help Cassandra better appreciate how readers would react to her instructions. She should focus more on what her readers need to know about a topic, instead of trying to share all the information she knows about it.

2. Students' answers will vary. An example answer follows: Karl should identify and consider the needs of his coworkers and help them understand how the planned speakers meet their needs. He also needs to choose speakers and topics with the employees' needs in mind, rather than just emphasizing recent research in the field.

Career Case Studies

Communication for Human and Social Services Careers

1. At least two answers are possible. Some students may point out that Katha is explaining the problem from the federal government's point of view, not the viewpoint of the intended readers. Students might also note that the letter stresses the negative things that will happen if the program participants do not improve instead of focusing on what they can gain from the program.

2. In the revision of her letter, Katha needs to emphasize how the program meets the readers' needs. Few people are motivated by a list of federal requirements or by the possible loss of a program they are not attending. Instead, Katha must focus on the readers' need to have jobs that will enable them to provide for themselves and their families. She should stress the benefits that the readers will gain from this program, including the basic work skills taught in the class and the specific skills they learn on the job.

    Katha might encourage the program participants to call her about any obstacles they have encountered in attending the program, such as a need for childcare or transportation. As supporting information, she might share success stories from former program participants. Katha must emphasize her primary appeal: The participants should continue in the program because it will help them to get and keep a good job.

Communication for Media and Visual Arts Careers

In the newsletter, Phil should write a description of the online service for teachers. It should be more of a process description, not a set of instructions, as most readers will not be following the steps to access the service. To help create goodwill in the community and avoid annoying readers with a library service that they cannot use, Phil should stress how this service will benefit local school children. He might also explain the specific steps in obtaining a PIN and accessing the service.

To meet the needs of teachers with varying computer knowledge, Phil might boldface the main steps in the instructions, so computer-adept teachers can skim them. He could add detailed instructions under each step for those teachers who have less experience in accessing and using online services.

Video Case

1. Students might argue that Pamela is overstating the effect of poor communication on New Tech's business but should acknowledge serious documentation deficiencies at New Tech. Students who believe that Pamela did not overstate the effect of poor communication on New Tech could cite Pamela's opinion of New Tech's internal and external documentation. After all, Pamela found unclear assembly instructions, quality control procedures with poor organization and few illustrations, and customer service reps using manuals written for an expert audience.

2. Students might suggest a glossary or good organization or a structure that divides the manual into chapters or sections. They might also suggest that the manual needs to be clear, well organized, appropriate for the intended readers, and inviting to the reader. Other students might cite the need for a clear and limiting title, a list of materials required, special skills required, a time frame, cautions, and clearly delineated steps.

3. Students should show evidence of planning a persuasive letter: identifying the objective and main idea, determining the supporting information, and adjusting the content to the reader.

4. Students should be able to separate examples of *persuasive* writing from *informational* writing or *instructional* writing on the web page. They might also comment on the direct or indirect way the manufacturer tries to convince the buyer.

Continuing Case

1. A first-stage collection letter should gently remind customers to pay a past-due bill.

2. Possible underlying messages: You are not a valued customer. You might cause our business to fail. Implied threat: You cannot continue to use our services until you pay your bill.

3. Students' rewritten reminder-stage letters should be short, friendly, polite, and in the direct order. They should not attack or insult the customers.

4. Students' strong-reminder-stage letters should be more pointed, but still not insulting. They should be direct, asking customers to pay the bill without threatening them. The amount of the overdue payment should be stated. Students might also describe some benefits of paying the bill, such as bringing the account up to date and preserving the customer's credit rating.

5. Answers will vary but the steps in the process should be similar to the following:
   (a) The steps of NetCafe's collection process are:
      (1) On the first day of the month, Eva sends out bills to credit customers and indicates that payments are due by the 20th.
      (2) If payments are not received by the end of the month, Eva sends the customer a reminder.
      (3) Eva waits for another two weeks, and if no payment is received she sends the customer a strong-reminder-stage collection letter.
   (b) Answers will vary but should contain reasons for choosing a list, an oral presentation, or both. Choosing both shows that students are thinking "outside the box." The best answer would be that receivers will understand the process if a presentation using a list is given.

6. Answers will vary. The newsletter should be in two-column format and should include a title, a date, and at least two articles.

Chapter 12
Presentations and Meetings

Student Learning Objectives

Section 1
- Describe two types of short oral presentations.
- Discuss planning, organizing, and outlining a formal presentation.
- Describe three important factors in delivering speeches.

Section 2
- Identify guidelines for effective participation in meetings.
- Organize a productive meeting.
- Discuss guidelines for leading a meeting effectively.

Teaching Outline

Introductory Points
- Oral communication is a common business activity.
- Types of oral communication you will be required to make depend upon your career.
- The higher you move up in a company, the more oral presentations you will be asked to make.
- Meetings are important because people use them to judge your abilities and competencies.
- Even in the most ordinary meeting, what you say and how you say it demonstrate your readiness for more responsibility or less.

I. Oral Presentations
  A. Short Oral Presentations
    1. Introducing speakers
      a. Obtain information about speakers
      b. Introduce speakers and their presentations
    2. Briefings

  B. Formal Oral Presentations
    1. Planning the presentation
      a. Determine the objective
      b. Analyze the audience (Use Transparency 12-1 for a review of the questions presenters should ask themselves to complete an audience analysis.)
      c. Determine time available
      d. Gather information
      e. Determine mode of delivery
    2. Organizing the presentation
      a. Introduction
        i. Quotations
        ii. Anecdotes
        iii. Humor
        iv. Statistics
        v. Questions
      b. Body
      c. Closing
    3. Outlining the presentation (Figure 12-1 illustrates a direct-order and an indirect-order outline. Ask students what makes one outline direct and the other indirect —Answer: the position of the presentation's main idea.)
  C. Delivery of Oral Presentations (Use Transparency 12-2 as a means to review techniques students can use to deliver their speeches well—overcome the fear of public speaking.)
    1. Voice qualities
    2. Nonverbal symbols
      a. Eye contact
      b. Facial expression
      c. Gestures
      d. Posture
    3. Visual aids
    4. Feedback (Use the checklist on page 418 as a means of reviewing the important aspects of an oral presentation.)

II. Effective Meetings
  A. Guidelines for Effective Participation in Meetings (Ask students to think of the worst meeting they have ever attended. Then ask them to identify what made that meeting so bad. Ask students to think of the best meeting they have ever attended. Then ask them what made that meeting so good. Use Figure

12-2 as a teaching tool for responsibilities and failures of meeting participants.)
1. Arrive on time
2. Participate actively
3. Improve decision making
4. Make a positive impact (Use Transparency 12-3 as a means of reviewing the concepts involved when trying to make a positive impact in a meeting.)
   a. Take a position but be willing to change it
   b. Speak briefly and directly
   c. Discuss ideas
   d. Avoid personal attacks
   e. Engage in fair play
   f. Use body language to your advantage
   g. Take notes
B. Organize Productive Meetings
1. Define the tasks
2. Determine the type of meeting
   a. To inform (Use Figure 12-3 to teach the important aspects of a meeting to inform.)
   b. To develop new ideas
   c. To make decisions (Use Figure 12-4 to teach the important aspects of a meeting to decide.)
   d. To delegate work
   e. To collaborate
   f. To persuade others
3. Choose participants carefully
4. Use the mechanics of an effective meeting
   a. Schedule meetings carefully
   b. Select an appropriate meeting site
   c. Arrange furniture appropriately
C. Lead Meetings Effectively
1. Begin effectively
2. Use an agenda
3. Stay focused on the task or objective
4. Balance the discussion
5. Make meetings successful
   a. Recognize contributions
   b. Maintain high standards
   c. Maintain order
6. End effectively (Use Transparency 12-4 as a tool to review the responsibilities of a leader of a meeting.)

Classroom Strategies

Many people fear public speaking, so it is important to emphasize to students that they *can* give effective oral presentations. Preparation and practice help speakers gain confidence. Encourage students to use the preparation checklist provided in the chapter.

Emphasize the importance of meetings to students—that they are avenues to promotion. Help students realize that each meeting has a purpose and that attendees should perform accordingly. When teaching about meetings, help students realize that there are three roles—participant, leader, and organizer. The chapter is structured to help them understand the responsibilities that go with each role.

Solutions to End-of-Section Activities

Discussion Questions

Section 12.1

1. Briefings and introductions are alike in that they are both short presentations and should be simple. They begin with an introduction that should get the audience's attention and prepare the audience for what is to come. They differ that in an introduction, the person making the introduction should talk with the person he or she is to introduce and make the introduction effective. In a briefing, the person giving the briefing probably already has the data for the presentation.

2. The two main reasons for planning and organizing oral presentations are
   a. When most of us have to give an oral presentation, we become nervous. Being organized and having a distinct plan will help us relax when delivering the presentation.
   b. By planning and organizing our oral presentations, we increase the probability that the presentation will be accepted by our audience.

Section 12.2

1. Yes, agendas are important in both long and short meetings. In both situations, agendas help the meeting participants stay on the topic and save time. They also reveal to participants the type of meeting that is being held.

2. Yes, the mechanics of a meeting are important. The meeting time, the meeting place, and appropriately arranged furniture make significant contributions to the effectiveness of a meeting. Not to consider these three elements of a meeting can cause it to fail.

Solutions to End-of-Chapter Activities

Critical Thinking Questions

1. Yes. In almost every job, you will have to attend meetings. How you conduct yourself at these meetings will send a nonverbal message about you. If you desire to move above an entry-level position, your conduct at meetings will help you advance in your career.
2. Probably. If you desire to move above an entry-level position, presentations may become part of your work. For example, if you become a department head or a supervisor, you will have to hold meetings of the department or group. However, if you do not desire to move above an entry-level position, then in some situations, you may never be asked to make an oral presentation.

Applications

Part A. Students' answers will vary.

Part B. Students' answers will vary.

Part C. Students' answers will vary but should focus on the presenter and the report. Areas that should be discussed under the presenter are appearance, eye contact, voice, posture, and originality or creativity. The areas that should be discussed under the report are presenter's knowledge of the topic, purpose of the report, effectiveness of the opening, effectiveness of the closing, and clarity of the report.

Part D. Students' answers will vary.

Part E. Students' answers will vary.

Part F. Students' answers will vary.

Part G. Students' answers will vary.

Part H. Students' answers will vary but should be in the form of a checklist. Items on the checklist should include the following three areas:

1. Organizing productive meetings—define the task, determine the type of meeting, and choose participants carefully
2. Mechanics for organizing a meeting—schedule meetings carefully, select an appropriate meeting site, and arrange the furniture appropriately
3. Effective leadership—begin effectively, use an agenda, stay focused on the objective, balance the discussion, make the meeting successful (recognize contributions, maintain high standards, and maintain order), and end effectively

Part I. Students' answers will vary.

Part J. Students' answers will vary but should include the answers to these questions: (1) Did participants arrive on time? (2) Did they actively participate? (3) Did they improve the decision making? (4) Did they make a positive impact on the meeting?

Editing Activities

[Corrected words and phrases are underlined.]

1. Yesterday, I <u>chose</u> to enroll in my <u>employer's</u> health insurance program. The two major <u>effects</u> of this decision <u>are</u> that (1) <u>the</u> cost of this insurance is <u>consistent</u> with what I can afford, and (2) the coverage of this policy will <u>fulfill</u> my <u>family's</u> needs. By <u>joining</u> this program, I am better able to <u>fulfill</u> the needs of my family.
2. Did you see the brochure and <u>pamphlet</u> on the <u>South</u> Seas? They were extraordinary. <u>They had</u> pictures of <u>unique</u> waterfalls, beaches, and hotels. Sarah is <u>planning</u> to go <u>there</u> on her vacation. I wish I <u>were</u> going with her. However<u>,</u> this year, because of a lack of funds, my family and I will be going to the <u>mountains</u>. We will be camping out in tents (<u>no comma here</u>) and enjoying nature at <u>its</u> best.

Case Studies

1. Students' answers will vary. However, they should include (1) how Toastmasters' International works, (2) how to join, (3) the location of the club nearest you, and (4) ten tips on presenting speeches.

The explanation of how Toastmasters' works could include tools provided to members, content on Toastmasters' and its leadership, and the benefits it offers you, your employer, and your community. Content on becoming a member is divided into how to find a club and how to start a club. The answers to the club nearest you will vary. Tips for speaking should include (1) know your room, (2) know your audience, (3) know your material, (4) relax, (5) visualize yourself giving your speech, (6) realize that people want you to succeed, (7) don't apologize, (8) concentrate on the message—not the medium, (9) turn nervousness into positive energy, and (10) gain experience.

2. Terry's memo should include the following three areas:

   a. Organizing productive meetings—define the task, determine the type of meeting, and choose participants carefully

   b. Mechanics for organizing a meeting—schedule meetings carefully, select an appropriate meeting site, and arrange the furniture appropriately

   c. Effective leadership of meetings—begin effectively, use an agenda, stay focused on the objective, balance the discussion, make the meeting successful (recognize contributions, maintain high standards, and maintain order), and end effectively

Career Case Studies

Communication for Engineering and Industrial Careers

1. Students' answers will vary, but they should be similar to those below.

   Areas that need to be covered in the presentation are

   a. An attention-getting introduction
   b. The plan
      (1) the financial benefits to production-line workers, middle management, and the company
      (2) how employees can submit an idea
      (3) how they will be notified of the results of their submission
   c. Enthusiastic action-seeking ending

2. Yes, audience analysis should have an impact on my presentation. I should adjust the content of my presentation to ensure that all employees

understand it. I should also consider how they will view the plan and adjust my presentation so that they will respond to it enthusiastically.

3. Yes, I would use visual aids to break up the presentation and for points of emphasis such as possible dollar benefits to middle management and production-line employees.

Communication for Media and Visual Arts Careers

1. Students' answers will vary. A possible solution is as follows:

   I would do nothing special. I would clean and prepare the center as I would for any other day. To prepare it for the visit by giving it an especially good cleaning would make it look better than it normally does and decrease the possibility of receiving funding. To make it look worse than it usually does so that funding is more apt to be granted would be unethical. To do nothing special gives the visitors a realistic view of what the public sees when they come to this state-funded center.

2. Students' answers will vary. A possible solution is as follows:

   One special thing that I might do is make sure there is a sign in the entry stating that this center is state funded. Hopefully, this action would put pressure on the visitors because they would not want a state-funded center to look run down.

Video Case

1. The speech is largely persuasive. It focuses on Sam's experience as a hemophiliac and his characterization of blood donors as "healers." Students may note informative elements: the safety or ease of giving blood or the rapidity with which the body begins regenerating blood. Perceptive students might argue that the speech was mainly persuasive and that information sections were used only to break down resistance to giving blood.

2. Sam uses humor to introduce what some might find an uncomfortable topic. He tries to make eye contact with all members of the audience. He shares his personal experience to make blood donation less of an abstract concept. He speaks at a good pace for understanding and uses a calm, but sincere, tonal quality. He uses statistics to reinforce his points.

3. Presentations will vary. Students should be able to categorize their presentations as either informative or persuasive, and the support material they select should support that tone. The amount of graphics should support the theme without providing too many breaks in the flow of the presentation. Students sometimes struggle to find a balance between too many and too few graphics.

Continuing Case

1. It should be in the indirect order because of Dominic's possible rejection of their plans to open a new branch.
2. Possible attention-getters: statistics about how much profit the NetCafe has made and other evidence of its success; a joke, perhaps about old friends and money; an anecdote about something funny that happened at the shop.

3. Possible topics: how much profit the current shop made each quarter; which services are most profitable at this point; potential earnings for the third year in Milwaukee; the reasons for setting up a new shop in Chicago (from a business point of view); a description of the chosen location and its advantages; possible competition for the NetCafe in Chicago; staffing plans for Milwaukee and Chicago; a tentative schedule for opening the new shop; the services it will offer; the amount of capital needed to open the new shop; potential gains for investors in the shop.
4. The exact order of the topics will vary. However, students should put them in indirect order, talking first about the successes in Milwaukee, leading to the new shop in Chicago, and ending with a request for support for the new shop.
5. Students will give their presentations.

Chapter 13
Communicating with Customers

Student Learning Objectives

Section 1
- Explain the importance of customer service.
- Identify external and internal customers.
- Explain the qualities of courteous, professional customer contact.
- Describe the appropriate way to receive customers.
- Discuss the importance of using ethical behavior when dealing with customers.
- Explain how to use communication technology in communicating effectively with customers.

Section 2
- Recognize vocal qualities that are most helpful to productive communication.
- Describe the factors that lead to successful one-on-one communication.
- Identify techniques for communicating effectively on the telephone.

Teaching Outline

Introductory Points
- All workers are responsible for customer service, even if they don't have direct contact with customers.
- Taking care of internal customers is at least as important as taking care of external customers.
- One-on-one and telephone communication each require special skills.

I. Customer Service
   A. Why Is Quality Customer Service So Important?
   1. More companies compete for consumers' attention.
   2. Quality customer service is often the difference between two companies providing similar products or services.

   B. External and Internal Customers
   1. External customers are people from outside a company who request information or purchase a service or product.
   2. Internal customers are a worker's coworkers, supervisors, and colleagues.
   3. Treating *all* customers courteously and providing accurate information in a tactful manner ensures external and internal customer satisfaction.

   C. Customer Service and Contact
   1. Maintain adequate customer contact by means of telephone calls, e-mail, faxes, and so on, to ensure customer satisfaction.
   2. Be accessible to customers and respond promptly to all forms of communication.
   3. Give knowledgeable responses and follow up with explanations or further information if necessary.
   4. Maintain continuous contact with a customer until that customer is satisfied. (Use Transparency 13-1.)
   5. Follow company policies and procedures for customer service.
   6. A company with a strong service culture empowers its service providers to take whatever steps necessary to ensure customer satisfaction.

   D. Customer Interaction
   1. Customers form impressions the moment they enter the presence of a customer service provider, and those impressions must be favorable.
   2. Give customers prompt attention, even if it is just to acknowledge their presence.
   3. A cheerful greeting can set the tone for the rest of a service provider's contact with a customer.
   4. Customer service providers should provide courteous, professional service regardless of how they feel or how the customer behaves.
   5. Use active listening so customers know you understand what they're saying and that you care.
   6. Determine each customer's needs; don't assume.
   7. Apologize, without laying blame, if an error occurs; then rectify the error.

8. Use tact and discretion, particularly when dealing with sensitive or confidential issues such as finances or health care. (Use Transparency 13-2.)

E. Customer Service and Ethics
1. Communicate in an ethical manner by providing accurate, complete information.
2. Communicate ethically by maintaining confidentiality.
3. Many companies, organizations, and professions have a code of ethics that employees or members are expected to follow.

F. Technology and Effective Communication with Customers
1. Telecommunications allow personal contact even over long distances.
2. Voice mail allows people to leave personal, recorded messages even if someone is not at home or in the office.
3. Cellular phones and pagers keep people in touch whether they are in or out of the office. (Use Transparency 13-3.)
   a. Observe rules of etiquette when using cellular phones and pagers.
   b. Do not speak on a cellular phone or refer to a pager without first excusing yourself from your current customer's presence.
4. Use facsimile machines to transmit printed documents that contain tabular information, charts, or other graphics.
5. E-mail is a quick but less personal way to communicate with customers. (Critique Transparency 13-4.)
6. The Internet and the World Wide Web can be useful customer service tools.
7. The use of technology should not completely replace personal contact with customers, colleagues, or clients.

II. One-on-One and Telephone Communication
A. Communication and Your Voice
1. The quality of the human voice varies in terms of pitch, volume, and tone.
2. Vocal clarity involves enunciating—speaking clearly—and pronouncing—speaking words correctly.

B. One-on-One Communication
1. One-on-one communication is the most complex form of communication.

2. Using and interpreting body language appropriately are vital to communicating effectively one-on-one.
3. All conversations follow a pattern of five stages.
   a. Greeting
   b. Introduction
   c. Exchange
   d. Summary
   e. Closing
4. Certain guidelines can help you succeed in your one-on-one communication. (Use Transparency 13-5.)
   a. Relax.
   b. Think before you speak.
   c. Listen carefully—and actively.
   d. Use names.
   e. Use eye contact.
   f. Maintain a conversational, pleasant tone of voice.
   g. Be honest and sincere.

C. Telephone Communication
1. Telephone communication requires especially good listening skills because callers and recipients have only verbal cues, not visual cues, on which to rely.
2. Successful telephone communication depends on some preparation and clear thinking. (Use Transparency 13-6.)
   a. Plan calls.
   b. Identify yourself and your organization.
   c. Use a pleasant, low tone of voice.
   d. Speak clearly and courteously.
   e. Take messages accurately.
   f. Transfer calls efficiently.
   g. Close conversations cordially.

Classroom Strategies

Tell students that all of the communication skills they have already learned about are especially important when communicating with customers because their jobs and the success of their companies depend on the effectiveness of those skills. Emphasize the concept of internal customers. Point out that even as students they have internal customers. Those customers include faculty members, administrative staff, classmates, landlords or dormitory personnel, and so on. Have students treat everyone on campus as an internal customer for a week. Then ask them if their interactions were different because of their new attitude.

Draw on students' experiences as customers and as customer service providers to enhance the study of this chapter. As students offer their own experiences, help them analyze what should or should not have been done. Help them see how their own behavior, both as customers and as service providers, affects the outcome of events.

Role-playing is an effective way to show students what effective customer service looks like. Students are likely to recognize the obvious signs of good customer service. Role plays can help with the less obvious, such as tone of voice, posture, and attitude.

Solutions to End-of-Section Activities

Discussion Questions

Section 13.1

1. The purpose of customer service is to satisfy customers in such a way that all of their needs are met and they remain loyal, which helps to ensure their continuing business. Students' personal experiences with customer service will vary.
2. The initial impression a company or an employee makes on a customer is very important. It may determine whether that person becomes a customer or just a passerby. Students' opinions about the most important aspects of initial contact will vary.
3. There is less one-on-one contact with customers. People can carry out business on the telephone and by e-mail. This situation makes communication less personal, but customer service providers still need to supply quality service that is pleasant and helpful. Students may characterize the changes as positive or negative.

Section 13.2

1. Our voices have the qualities of pitch, volume, and tone. All three of those qualities combine to make our voices pleasant or unpleasant to listen to. How we use our voices affects how people view us.
2. Answers will vary. Students might list plan ahead, make eye contact, or smile, for example. Whatever the students suggest should pertain to preparing for the encounter or making a good first impression on the customer.
3. The receiver does not have the benefit of non-verbal cues, such as the caller's posture, facial ex-

pression, or gestures. Therefore, the caller's speech must be clear so that the receiver can acquire all of the message as accurately as possible.

Solutions to End-of-Chapter Activities

Critical Thinking Questions

1. Competition is increasing because there are more and more companies offering services to customers. Providing excellent customer service is a way for a company to distinguish itself among its competitors.
2. Continuous contact means staying in touch with a customer so that he or she never has to wonder what is happening. It involves keeping the customer informed about changes or developments in the business being conducted. Continuous contact reassures a customer that the service provider is attentive and doing a good job.
3. Service providers should use *all* of their communication skills. Communication is the key to being a good customer service provider. Service providers, as senders, must listen actively, speak coherently and appropriately, write in an organized and logical manner, and interpret receivers' feedback. Not making use of any or all of these skills prevents a service provider from providing quality customer service.
4. Failure to be honest, to disclose all information, or to observe a customer's right to confidentiality are all unethical behaviors.
5. They can use pagers, cellular phones, and voice mail to make themselves more accessible to customers. Customer service providers should use technology efficiently to enhance customer service, not to replace the sort of personal customer service that stands out in an increasingly technology-oriented society.

Applications

Part A. Help students evaluate customer service experiences objectively, based on the criteria suggested in this chapter. Students may need help identifying what caused them to form their impressions. Point out that tone of voice and attitude are often behind the impressions we form, even if the service provided is appropriate.

Part B. Students' answers will vary but should summarize a customer-service telephone conversation and evaluate it.

Part C.
1. The customer service provider must remember to make eye contact with the customer, not get absorbed in his or her computer screen. Because the customer is a senior citizen, the service provider should be especially respectful. Of course, because the transaction involves financial information, the service provider should maintain a low, confidential tone of voice.
2. The customer service provider must lay out exactly what she will do, and when, to get customers a replacement floor installed as quickly as possible. This would be one time when a call to the office on a cellular phone would be appropriate so that the customers can see the action begin right away.

Part D.
1. Students are likely to label this situation as clearly unethical. The technician takes the easy way out with his recommendation to the customer. The customer will end up with a whole new motor assembly, but it would cost him less if the technician just fixed the broken parts. The technician does not give the customer that option.
2. This situation is a little less clear than the previous situation; students' answers may vary. At the basic level, the practice is somewhat unfair in that the store is not making as wide a range of choices available to its customers. As long as the store doesn't advertise the basic models, then claim that they are unavailable once customers come into the store (a practice called *bait and switch*), the store's actions are probably not unethical.

Part E. Students' answers will vary.

Part F. Answers will vary but discussion should involve the essential elements of each conversation.

Editing Activity

Corrected words or phrases are underlined.

The instructions on the <u>conference</u> registration <u>form</u> asked attendees to express their first, second, and third choices for housing. <u>You</u> listed only one choice on the form, and that hotel is full. Please reply via e-mail today so that I may know your further preferences. If I <u>don't</u> hear from you, I will have to assign you to <u>whatever</u> housing is left.

Case Studies
1. a. This role-play should involve just the young employee and the customer. Note that the whole encounter is quite brief, yet the customer forms an impression, does not receive any offer of further assistance, and leaves.
   b. The supervisor's statements should be constructive; they should not be patronizing or disciplinary in nature. The supervisor's goal is to educate and train, not to punish. The advice should have to do with attitude and with trying to be helpful, even if a customer makes a request that the employee can't exactly fulfill.
   c. In this scene, the employee's response to the customer's initial request must be more explicit. If the computer matching system won't work, perhaps there is another way to help the customer match her color.
2. All of the web sites listed are fairly complex and well maintained. Students will have to evaluate the sites critically because all of them have much to offer. Encourage students to consider what makes one site preferable to another in terms of the customer service each site provides.

Career Case Studies

Communication for Health Services
1. Students' plans should take into consideration the needs of well and sick children and their parents. Suggestions and features may include the following: separate well and sick waiting rooms; a reception area from which staff can acknowledge arriving parents and where parents can converse reasonably privately with a receptionist or nurse; a separate desk or counter for paying bills and dealing with insurance issues; distractions for children such as a chalk board, video viewing area, books, or other toys. Decorating schemes should be child-oriented, but should also be soothing and relaxing.
2. Students' answers will vary.
3. Students' answers will vary.
4. Students' answers will vary.

Communication for Human and Personal Services
1. Students' answers will vary.
2. Students' suggestions will vary. Indirectly, Jan could conduct some training for the whole staff, so as not to single out Steve. She could leave some leaflets in the break room for her employ-

ees to read. If Jan wants or needs to act directly, she will have to explain to Steve the concept of internal customers. She could draw on his good sense of external customer service to get the point across. In any case, the situation is sensitive because it has to do with an employee's personality. The challenge is to address the issue from a behavioral standpoint. That will reduce the likelihood of offending Steve.

Video Case

1. Boyd's employees are encouraged to make the extra effort to provide excellent service to their clients. As one employee said, "The goal is to show customers, 'You're not only paying for the product, you're paying for the service as well.'" Students might also cite customers praising Boyd and his staff as the truest sign of what customer service means to this company.

2. Possible answers:
   DO's
   - Greet the customer cheerfully.
   - Watch tone, pitch, and clarity of voice.
   - Use careful pronunciation.
   - Include a greeting, introduction, and summary.
   - Remain relaxed.
   - Listen carefully.

   DON'T's
   - Don't speak too fast or mumble.
   - Don't interrupt.
   - Don't assume you know what a customer wants.
   - Don't be afraid to issue a simple apology.
   - Don't be afraid to say "I don't know."
   - Don't guess when giving customers information.

3. Answers will vary, but they should incorporate the guidelines from Chapter 6 on writing letters with a negative message. For example, the letter's organization should include a neutral opening, an explanation of the reason for the negative news, a statement of the negative news, and a closing on a positive note.

Continuing Case

1. Yes, because meeting customers' needs is essential for the NetCafe.

2. Yes, because the new shop will fail unless there are enough customers who want the services offered by NetCafe and cannot get them elsewhere.

3. Students' responses to Questions (a) and (b) will vary, but they should be logical and thoughtful. Below are possible responses.
   a. A discount on NetCafe services; a free cup of coffee; the addition of or a change in a service
   b. A printed survey questionnaire that customers fill out in the store might be best. Customers who pay cash would not receive the questionnaire in a monthly bill. The NetCafe is not likely to have every customer's e-mail address.
   c. Students' answers should incorporate the standards described in the chapter, including accessibility, knowledgeable responses, clear policies and procedures, prompt and courteous attention, confidentiality, and ethical conduct.
   d. Students' surveys should include clearly worded questions or statements, grouped and labeled by categories. They should also devise a rating scale, such as the one below.

never	occasionally	usually	often	always
1	2	3	4	5

4. Again, students' responses will vary. Below are some possibilities.
   a. A discount on services; free cup of coffee; the offering of a service they really want.
   b. The survey questionnaire might be mailed or hand-delivered to businesses and homes (apartment buildings) in the area; it might be posted on the NetCafe web site, perhaps with a notice in local papers urging potential customers to log on and complete it.
   c. The survey questionnaire should be short, no more than one page, to encourage people to complete it. It might list services that could be offered by the NetCafe and ask customers to mark the ones they think are essential, plus others they would like to have. The questionnaire might also ask how likely the person is to visit the NetCafe and how often those visits might occur.

Chapter 14
Employment Communication

Student Learning Objectives

Section 1
- Analyze your personal and career goals.
- Identify your qualifications.
- Analyze the job market.
- Research potential employers.

Section 2
- Describe how to organize and prepare a resume.
- Understand the opportunities provided by electronic resumes.

Teaching Outline

Introductory Points
- The job search is an exciting but challenging time.
- Begin your job search at least three months before you want to start work.
- Only if you know your personal and career goals and are aware of job opportunities are you ready to start your search for employment.
- Frequently, a resume will be quickly scanned to determine if the applicant has the necessary qualities and skills for a job. If it passes, it will be looked at again at a later date.
- Appearance and correctness many times gets your resume through the quick scanning phase.

I. Analyzing Yourself and the Market (Ask students, "How can you find a job that you really enjoy?" Answer: By doing a thorough self-analysis. Stress that a self-analysis is critical to their finding that "right" job.)
   A. Your Job Search
      1. Personal goals
      2. Career goals
   B. Analyze Your Qualifications
      1. Work experience
      2. Education
      3. Achievements and activities
      4. Special skills and personal traits
   C. Analyze the Job Market
      1. Identifying job openings
         a. School placement offices
         b. Personal contacts
         c. Newspapers and professional publications
         d. Internet
         e. Employment agencies
         f. Temp agencies or temp services
      2. Internships
      3. Libraries
   D. Research Specific Organizations (Use Transparency 14-1 to help students identify the information they need to gather on each company.)
      1. Conduct your research
      2. Organize your research
II. Writing Your Resume
   A. Organizing Your Resume
      1. Reverse chronological order (Use Figure 14-2 to teach students how to use this order when writing resumes.)
      2. Functional order (Use Transparency 14-2 to teach students how to use this order when writing resumes.)
   B. Preparing Your Resume (Stress that the content of a resume evolves over a period of time and that students must stay up-to-date or the content of their resume may not be appropriate.)
      1. Heading
      2. Job objective
      3. Special qualifications
      4. Work experience
      5. Education
      6. Activities, interests, and achievements
      7. Personal information
      8. References
      9. Emphasize that certain parts of a resume are optional (job objective, personal information, and references) and that the other parts are not optional. If students have no data to place in the required parts of a resume, employers will probably perceive those job seekers to be lacking.

C. Creating Electronic Resumes
1. Scannable resumes (Point out that the resume example in Figure 14-2 is a scannable resume.)
2. On-line resumes (Use Figure 14-3 to show students the first page of an on-line resume. Explain to them how buttons on the first page work.)

Classroom Strategies

When teaching this chapter, it is important to stress that while the activities covered in Chapter 14 (self-analysis, market analysis, and resume writing) are just the first part of getting a job that will make students happy, they are critical. Use the saying, "He who has no goals ends up somewhere." In other words, if students do not take the time to identify what makes them happy and where these jobs are located, they will "end up somewhere."

Indicate to students that only after completing the self-analysis and market analysis are they ready to write their resumes. Emphasize that the self-analysis helps them to understand themselves and the skills, talents, and abilities they have to offer employers. The market analysis helps students to recognize the skills, talents, and abilities particular employers are looking for in prospective employees. This information is critical to the student when attempting to write an effective resume for a particular job opening. Stress that this chapter will help students recognize what should and should not be placed on a resume.

Solutions to End-of-Section Activities

Discussion Questions

Section 14.1
1. The job-getting process begins with self-analysis because prospective workers need to understand themselves. Only then can they find jobs and work that they enjoy.
2. The areas of self-analysis can vary, depending upon the individual, but the basic areas that should be included are personal goals, career goals, qualifications, work experience, education, achievements and activities, and special skills and personal traits.

3. Market analysis is an important part of your job search. It helps you identify job openings and companies in which you would have a good chance to enjoy your work.

Section 14.2
1. The two basic orders for resumes are the reverse chronological order and the functional order. These two orders are used because they help you present your qualifications in the most positive way possible. Other orders are possible, but create them only if they enable you to present your qualifications more effectively than the basic two orders.
2. There are two basic advantages of an on-line resume over a traditional one-page resume.
    a. The on-line resume gives its writer much broader exposure. Because it is electronic, the on-line resume can be pulled up any place the Web is available.
    b. The on-line resume allows the writer to present more of his or her qualifications than are appropriate in a traditional resume. The on-line resume does not restrict the writer to one page of content. An on-line resume also enables the web user to pick the qualification areas he or she wants to read with no time wasted.

Solutions to End-of-Chapter Activities

Critical Thinking Questions
1. The job-getting process is difficult for the following reasons:
    a. It is pressure packed—one mistake could cost you the job you want; while you are job hunting, you might encounter financial pressure because of a lack of income.
    b. It is complex—you can never prepare for some of the questions you may be asked.
    c. It is sometimes too long—if you consider your job-getting process as "too long," you may become discouraged and start to question your skills and qualifications.
2. They are equally important. To find a position that you will enjoy requires that you understand yourself and what you want. To have these insights, you need to analyze yourself. Market analysis is necessary to find an opening or job that fits your wants and needs. The resume is the

sales tool you use to advertise your skills and qualifications for that job that you want. Failing to do either analysis well could result in your taking a job in which you will be unhappy. Failing to write an effective resume could result in your not being offered a job in which you would have been happy.

Applications

Part A. Student answers will vary.

Part B. Student answers will vary.

Part C. Student answers will vary.

Part D. Student answers will vary.

Part E. Student answers will vary.

Part F. Student answers will vary.

Part G. Student answers will vary.

Part H. Here is a possible reverse chronological resume for this Application exercise:

JOANNE LARSEN
94 North Elm Drive   Eugene, OR 97405-4627
(503) 555-3072

OBJECTIVE	To become a teacher's aide at Redwoods Elementary School.
SPECIAL QUALIFICATIONS	Experience developing and implementing reading programs for elementary school children.
EDUCATION	Associate degree, Elementary Education, May 2001, Southwestern Oregon Community College, Coos Bay, Oregon.
EXPERIENCE	
September 1999 to Present	Parent Volunteer. St. Rose Academy, Eugene, Oregon. Assisted classroom teachers with fourth- and fifth-grade students. Prepared weekly reading assignments and vocabulary quizzes. Created a new reading program for learning-disabled students.
September 1995 to September 1999	Library Volunteer. Eugene Public Library, Eugene, Oregon. Assisted children's librarian with young readers program. Developed reading contests, monitored progress toward reading goals, and worked with children to boost reading comprehension.

INTERESTS AND ACTIVITIES	• Member, St. Rose Academy • Member, Parent-Teacher Organization • Tutor, Literacy Volunteers of America
REFERENCES	Available on request

Part I. Student answers will vary.

Editing Activities

1. Answers will vary. One possible solution is on Transparency 14-3. Below is another possible solution.

Your company advertised for an administrative assistant in the December 9 edition of the *Weekly Herald*. When I complete my studies in the Business Technology program at Central States Community College this month, I will be qualified for this position. Please consider me an applicant.

While attending school full time, I worked part time as a secretary for Storrs Windows for over a year. In addition to my secretarial duties, I handled all payroll processing and petty cash. I also supervised one clerical employee.

As you can see from the enclosed resume, my education and work background fit your requirements. May I have an interview with you to explain my qualifications in more detail? You may reach me at 555-0172 on any weekday. I look forward to discussing the possibility of joining your staff.

2.

November **2002** to **Present**	**Assistant to** buyer of computers. Business Systems, Inc., Atlanta, Georgia. Assist in purchasing for **seven** computer stores, **negotiate** with **vendors**, and compute price changes. **Organize** classes for computer **training**. Arrange for auto rentals, **flight** schedules, and hotel **accomodations**.

Case Studies

1. Students' answers to this case will vary. However, the resume and letters should be formatted correctly and attractively. Grading

considerations should include formatting, appearance, grammar, punctuation, spelling, and tone.

2. The following is a possible answer to the second case. The answer should be a memo in the traditional format. It should also contain a footnote explaining the order (direct or indirect) the writer selected and why.

To: Jan Jones, Human Resources Director
From: Norice Johnson
Date: August 20, 20—
Subject: Recommendation Regarding the Applicant Howard Chin

Hiring Howard Chin as a manager of one of our markets would probably be a mistake. Although his resume lists strengths, it exemplifies too many weaknesses.

Strengths

His strengths are
1. He has two years' work experience in the industry.
2. He was an achiever in school.

Weaknesses

His weaknesses are
1. His career in the food market industry seems to be going backwards. He started out as a manager of a store, was then made a department manager of a store, and is now out of the industry.
2. Although he was an achiever in school, his resume is of questionable quality: (a) the use of *I* in the education section; (b) the lack of specifics about his work experience; (c) the lack of information about his degrees, especially what they are in; and (d) the mechanical mistakes in his resume (the use of % instead of spelling it out and the spelling of *technical*—part of the name of one the schools he attended).
3. The letter of application also reflects weak writing skills: (a) the opening sentence in his letter of application is weak; (b) he continues to misspell *technical*; (c) he confuses the usage of *quiet* and *quite*; and (d) he does not give details about his work experience or leadership skills that "were apparent."

   Based on these findings, I cannot recommend his hiring. Should you have any questions, please call me at extension 4923. Thanks for the opportunity to evaluate this candidate. It was good practical experience.

Footnote to the instructor—we used direct order because the message will be viewed by the receiver as routine. However, if you knew that the applicant was a friend of the human resources director, you would use indirect order. In that situation, the receiver would have considered the memo to contain bad news.

Career Case Studies

Communications for Engineering and Industrial Careers

1. Student answers will vary. However, the following is a possible answer. "I think Penelope is looking for someone who has a good speaking voice and someone who is polite, patient, competent, and helpful. She probably would like someone with experience as a receptionist."

2. Student answers will vary.

Communications for Business and Marketing Careers

1. Students' answers will vary, but a possible rewrite of the work experience section of his resume is:

Chanise's Hardware Store

Credit Manager
January 2002–present
- Evaluate customer credit applications.
- Counsel individuals on the use and abuse of credit.

Head of Electronics Department
February 1998–December 2001
- Arranged work schedule for electronics department personnel.
- Counted and maintained inventory for department.
- Resolved customer and personnel disputes.

Electronics Department Clerk
September 1995–January 1998
- Developed customer service skills.
- Received freight and kept stockroom clean.

2. Students should identify that his original work experience section was (1) wordy, which made it difficult to follow; (2) not organized in reverse chronological order; (3) not formatted properly;

(4) contained spelling errors; and (5) contained additional information not relevant to his work experience.

Continuing Case

1. The format is clear and easy to skim. However, the objective is poor, suggesting that Pat is too interested in being boss and offering no information about his or her field of expertise. The employment information is too brief and offers little to recommend Pat for this job. Pat should at least state how many staff he or she occasionally supervises and what kind of temporary assignments he or she has handled. Each "sentence" should begin with a strong verb.

2. This objective is poor, too, because it does not explain Terry's field of expertise/experience. The employment information implies that Terry was just passing through and not interested in food service. Terry should have explained why he or she was chosen as employee of the month. Terry's degree might make Eva wonder why he or she is not working in accounting or looking for a job in that field. Terry could have helped to answer this question in the job objective: "Seeking a position that will enable me to use my background in accounting and gain skills in management."

3. Students' responses will vary, but they should be logical and thoughtful. Whether Eva interviews Pat or Terry will depend to some degree on the quality of the other applicants. Both of these resumes are weak, however, and do not suggest that either candidate has the skills or background to manage the coffee counter.

Chapter 15
Job Application and Interviewing Skills

Student Learning Objectives

Section 1
- Describe two types of application letters.
- Describe the content of a letter of application.
- Fill in an application form.

Section 2
- Discuss the purpose of a job interview.
- Explain how to prepare for an interview.
- Understand the skills necessary for a successful interview.
- Write a follow-up letter.

Teaching Outline

Introductory Points
- The objective of the letter of application and resume is to get the writer an interview.
- The letter of application is a persuasive message and is written in the indirect order.
- The letter of application should be viewed as a sales tool.
- The application form is an important document and should be filled out as completely and neatly as possible.
- A successful interview gets you the job.
- The applicant can use the job interview to determine whether he or she wants to work for a particular company.

I. Application Letter
  A. Opening Paragraph
    1. Do points a, b, and c (below) in all openings. Do point d in the openings of unsolicited letters of application.
      a. Indicate that you are applying for a position.
      b. Name the position for which you are applying.
      c. Tell how you learned of the opening.
      d. In unsolicited letters of application, identify your abilities.
    2. Openings in solicited letters of application
      a. Identify the advertisement that told you of the opening.
      b. If a person told you of the opening, use his or her name—with his or her permission.
    3. Openings in unsolicited letters of application
      a. Focus on your abilities.
      b. Demonstrate your knowledge of the company's needs.
  B. Body Paragraphs
    1. If it is good, focus on your work experience.
    2. If you don't have much work experience, focus on your other strengths.
    3. Highlight the qualities that the employer likes or wants.
    4. If information on the resume might raise a question, explain it in the body of the letter of application.
  C. Closing Paragraph
    1. Avoid the overused phrase, "May I have an interview at your convenience?"
    2. Set a confident tone.
    3. Make it easy for the employer to contact you.
  D. Apply the General Guidelines for Letters of Application (see page 514 for the listing). (Use Transparency 15-1 to review solicited letters of application.)
  E. Fill Out Application Forms Appropriately
    1. Use sample application forms for practice.
    2. Use Transparency 15-2 for tips on filling out application forms.

II. Interviewing Well and Writing the Follow-up Letter
  A. The Purpose of the Job Interview
    1. To get the job
    2. To determine whether you want the job
  B. Preparing for the Interview
    1. Investigate the company and the job.
    2. Anticipate questions that might be asked during the interview—see the listing in Figure 15-4 on page 521 for common questions.
    3. Be prepared to ask questions—see the listing of this type of question on page 520.
    4. Practice for the interview.
    5. Bring appropriate information and items.
    6. Dress for the interview—see bulleted list on page 522.
    7. Arrive on time.
  C. The Interview Itself
    1. General concepts
      a. Avoid smoking.
      b. Avoid gum chewing.
      c. Greet the secretary cordially.
      d. Avoid bringing friends or relatives to the interview.
  D. Nonverbal Skills and Listening Skills—Use Transparency 15-3 to teach the nonverbal and listening skills needed in a successful interview.
  E. Interview Questions
    1. Opening questions help the interviewee relax.
    2. Main questions
      a. A simple yes or no is not enough—elaborate.
      b. Answer questions accurately.
    3. Illegal questions—review illegal questions by using Figure 15-5 on page 525.
    4. Avoid mentioning salary. However, if asked, indicate the standard salary for the position; this may require some research on the interviewee's part.
  F. The Closing
    1. The interviewer will provide both verbal and nonverbal signals that the interview is over.
    2. Thank the interviewer at the appropriate time.
  G. Follow-up Letter
    1. This letter is a goodwill letter.
    2. Thank the interviewer for the interview.
    3. Express continued interest in the position.
    4. Offer to send the interviewer any other needed information.

Classroom Strategies

Make this chapter as "real world" as possible. To select an advertisement from some source and write a cover letter for it and then be interviewed are two good activities. To videotape the interviews and then have students evaluate their interviews is another good activity. After the students have been interviewed, require them to write a follow-up letter to you thanking you for the interview.

Another good classroom strategy is to let students who have gone through the job-getting process tell of their experiences. Also, this would be a good time to have a guest speaker tell of the process he or she uses to select a candidate for a job and what causes that interviewer to reject some applicants.

Solutions to End-of-Section Activities

Discussion Questions

Section 15.1

1. They differ in the openings. In the solicited letter, the response is expected and should tell the receiver that the writer is applying for a position, the name of the position, and the source of the information about the opening. In the opening of the unsolicited letter, those same three items are given as well as characteristics of the candidate that make him or her qualified for the position.

2. Any letter format can be used in either type of letter of application. Their formats should not differ.

3. The application form is used by companies to gather additional information about candidates in whom they are seriously interested.

Section 15.2

1. The interview is probably more important than the follow-up letter. You can get a position without a follow-up letter; however, this type of letter can help a candidate obtain a job.

2. Employers interview applicants so they can identify the best candidate for the position. This process also allows candidates to determine whether they want to work for a company—lowering the company's turnover rate and costs.

3. To prepare for an interview, (1) investigate the company and opening, (2) anticipate questions, (3) be prepared to ask questions, (4) practice for the interview, (5) take appropriate information to the interview, (6) dress appropriately for the interview, and (7) arrive on time.

4. Candidates should send a follow-up letter to tell the company they are still interested in the position and to get their names before the interviewer again.

Solutions to End-of-Chapter Activities

Critical Thinking Questions

1. Both are important. The resume gets you the interview, but the interview gets you the job. Without either, you cannot get the job.

2. If the candidate sends a well-written follow-up letter, that candidate will have an advantage over a candidate who does not send one. However, if the candidate sends a poorly written follow-up letter, a candidate who does not send one will have the advantage.

Applications

Part A. Student answers will vary.

Part B. Student answers will vary.

Part C. Student answers will vary.

Part D. Student answers will vary.

Part E. Student answers will vary.

Editing Activities

[Corrected words are underlined.]

1. In WordPerfect, you can add a border or fill to a page or column. To do so, select the text you want to dress up. If you want to apply the effects to all your pages, paragraphs, or columns, don't select any text. Your formatting them affects all text from the insertion marker forward. Border options are found, appropriately enough, on the Border tab of the Border/Fill dialog box.

2. Thank you for taking time from your busy schedule to interview me for the position of assistant head teller. I also enjoyed the tour of your main branch.

   As I mentioned during the interview, your computerized account system is very impressive. Because it is similar to the one I use in my current position at Western Bank, I am sure I could adapt to it in only a few days.

   Given my years of experience with Western Bank, I would perform well and enjoy the challenge of serving the customers of Ansonia Savings Bank. If you need additional references or other information, please let me know.

Case Studies

1. Manuel should dress conservatively for all interviews. For the plumbers' position, khakis and a white shirt and tie are good. For the hospital position, a suit or a sports jacket, slacks, shirt, and tie would be acceptable.

   Manuel's questions should vary in detail but be basically the same. For example, if he were to ask about his work, he might say to the interviewer for the plumber position, "What type of plumber's work would I be expected to do?" For the hospital position, he might say, "What type of health care work would I be expected to do?"

2. In the solicited letter, the opening paragraph should tell the receiver that the writer is applying for a position, the name of the position, and the source of the information about the opening. In the opening paragraph of the unsolicited letter, those same three items are given as well as characteristics of the candidate that make him or her qualified for the position.

Sample solutions would be

I saw your advertisement for a person with a background in horticulture and two years' experience in the July 10 edition of the *Hillside Express*. Please consider me an applicant for this position. While studying horticulture at Hillside High, I learned many techniques to improve plant growth.

I saw your advertisement for a person with a background in horticulture and two years' experience in the July 10 edition of the *Hillside Express*. Please consider me an applicant for this position.

Career Case Studies

Communication for Media and Visual Arts Careers

1. Student answers will vary. Below is a possible response.

   First, I would tell him to relax. Being a little nervous is okay as long as it is used to ensure proper preparation. But being too nervous can cause an applicant to interview poorly.

   To prepare for an interview, I would tell Brandon to (1) investigate the station and the opening, (2) anticipate questions, (3) be prepared to ask questions, (3) practice for the interview, (4) take appropriate information to the interview, (5) dress appropriately for the interview, and (6) arrive on time.

2. Answers will vary.

Communication for Human and Social Services Careers

1. Student answers will vary. Below is a possible answer.

   LaQuanta should have been prepared and anticipated that she might be asked to fill out an application form. However, because she did not have all of the needed information, she should ask permission to take the form home and fill it out. If possible, she should key in the answers.

2. Student answers will vary. Below is a possible answer.

   LaQuanta should have been prepared to fill out an application form. She should have brought to the interview a blue or black ink pen, copies of her resume, and copies of her references list.

Continuing Case

1. Responses will vary. Below are some possibilities:
   a. Good question.
   b. Illegal; not possible to rephrase.
   c. Good question.
   d. Good question.
   e. Good question but should be rephrased so it cannot be answered by simply yes or no.
   f. Good question but should be rephrased to gather more information about the applicant's computer knowledge.
   g. Insulting to everyone; delete completely.
   h. Good question.
   i. Good question but should be rephrased so it cannot be answered by simply yes or no.
2. Students' resumes and letters of application for the manager's position will vary.
3. The order in which students place these characteristics will vary but should show some thought. Any new characteristics they add should be reasonable and relate closely to the position Eva is filling. Students should eliminate *physical fitness, youthful appearance,* and *stylishness of clothing* from the list. *Lack of nervousness* is another possible candidate for elimination but open to discussion.
4. Responses will vary. Below are some possibilities:
   a. Reason for concern: applicants should have done some homework before the interview.
   b. Good question.
   c. Reason for concern: applicants should not ask about benefits before being offered the job.
   d. Good question.
   e. Good question.
   f. Reason for concern: applicants should not ask about pay before being offered the job.
   g. Reason for concern: suggests an unwillingness to learn about computers; everyone at the NetCafe must be reasonably familiar with computers.
   h. Reason for concern: it may be difficult for someone to sell coffee who doesn't drink it.
   i. Good question.
   j. Good question.
   k. Reason for concern: the manager would be the logical person to handle problems; this person might not have a clear understanding of the job of a manager.

Appendix C Grammar and Mechanics

Solutions to End-of-Section Activities

Section 1

Applications

Part A. Students' sentences will vary.

Part B
1. hers
2. who
3. them
4. its
5. His

Part C
1. easier
2. smarter
3. well-known
4. incredibly
5. bad
6. most intelligently
7. really
8. that

Part D
1. among
2. besides
3. into
4. delete *at*
5. nor
6. Because
7. enthusiastically
8. no errors
9. Until
10. or

Editing and Proofreading Applications

I. months, greatly, affected, sudden, agents, more bitterly, than, their, commissions, fully, unexpected, assured, carefully, do, too severely, meanwhile, your, cautiously, daily, frequently, forward, rapid

II. in, have, business, about, opposite, at, newer, than, better, on, away, opening, regard, beneficial, over.

III. Students' answers will vary.

Section 2

Applications

Part A
1. actors
2. tellers, officers
3. Every one
4. Both
5. sister

Part B
1. has
2. have listened, have heeded
3. is
4. will scrape
5. enhances

Part C
1. have been offered
2. are
3. was
4. was
5. were
6. is
7. has found
8. plan

Part D
1. his or her seat
2. one expects
3. his or her mind
4. her or his side
5. their opinions
6. its bid
7. who suggested

Editing and Proofreading Applications

I. households, dependents, who, residents, of, their, recreational, already, received, these, already, questionnaire, families, who, years, construction, their, which, them, these, their, our

II. your, overcome, deficiency, has, February, is, provides, Here's, may elect, deductions, contribute, is applied, will receive, pays, receive, dividends, are, eligible, are, questionnaire, there, are

Section 3

Applications

Part A
1. ?
2. .
3. .
4. .
5. !

Part B
1. Therefore,
2. think, however,
3. doctor,
4. Clara,/whiz,
5. work,

Part C
1. window and
2. leave now
3. delete the commas
4. new navy blue
5. delete the comma

Part D
1. "The/Osaka,"/agent. "You/Kobe."
2. —80 miles.
3. men's suits, women's dresses,/children's/ inventoried.
4. week's/<u>Encyclopedia Atlas and Illustrations</u>.
5. Korea,/"What/America"?

Editing and Proofreading Applications

I. Now that/calmed/down,/justified/Friday./Being/ weekend does/fair/understand that/overtime/hours when/needed,/sons/were/old,/their/party. If/weeks/ June 7,/arranged/substitute or/notice, /was/ arrangements./Quenton,/supervisor,/further

II. apologize/forwarding/bill;/sincerely/you./10:15/ Tuesday?/then./forgetful—/overworked?/time;/ records./double-checked/mailed./spot-checked/ convenient/you. My/Small;/Alvarez;/months

III. I/interested/increasingly/phase/spoke/represen-tatives/"All/have/transferred/"How to Transfer Funds'." or <u>How to Transfer Funds</u>."/(Fidelity/Bank)/ mail/company./funds/haven't/"Because/administrator/ didn't/signature."/booklet/Apparently/funds./ recommend/"Not/time."

Section 4

Applications

Part A
1. South Carolina, North Carolina, year
2. YMCA, New York, organizations
3. Saturday, Sunday
4. January, account, balance
5. Dr., Mr.

Part B
1. Do, second, Office Equipment Association, California, April?
2. Spiegel, catalog, costs.
3. DC, Air and Space Museum, National Gallery of Art.
4. National Spelling Bee, "You, scholar."
5. Floridians, skiing, Colorado, surfing, Miami.

Part C
1. ordered, eight
2. two hundred, to
3. Eleven
4. will ship, eight, 200-volt
5. have, 6

Part D
1. 2005, our, Indianapolis
2. Respond, September 12, 1 percent
3. One, Munroe Street, accommodate
4. United States, has, $7 million
5. Representative, Twenty-second, District, supports

Editing and Proofreading Applications

I. Monday, August, procedures, mortgage, loan., Friday, balance, $694.00, account., don't, nuisance, questions:, account, balance, mortgage, balance, check, difference?, payment, New Jersey, where, mortgage, payment?

II. tenth OR 10th/visited/consultant/two/blouses/
one/receive/by/8/second/an/has/One/clothes/
arrived/eighteenth OR 18th/10/2003/were/
consultant/Two/are/October 1, 2003/off/your/
$535/straight/2/receive/half/yourself/your

Section 5

Applications

Part A

1. lie
2. Whether
3. elude
4. personnel
5. metal
6. too/loose
7. cite
8. your

Part B

1. capital/all together
2. passed/insured/principal
3. there/too
4. effect/fourth/its
5. counsel/any one/Corporation
6. complimented/desert
7. hear/envelopes/quite/stationery
8. assured/farther/than
9. no errors
10. chose/horde

Editing and Proofreading Applications

1. on 45 minutes' notice
2. a three-year-old horse
3. Here comes Mr. Jon Woolner!
4. an SBA disaster loan
5. a first edition Jane Austen novel
6. a Jewish holiday
7. the 24th of August
8. On page 329, 25 references apply.
9. Plese accept their apology.
10. how to effect a change